Families
in Pain

Other Books by Jack and Judith Balswick

The Dual-Earner Marriage: The Elaborate Balancing Act
The Family: A Christian Perspective on the Contemporary Home
Raging Hormones: What to Do When You Suspect Your Teen Might Be Sexually Active

Judith Balswick is associate professor of family therapy at Fuller Theological Seminary. Jack Balswick is professor of sociology and family development at Fuller Seminary and is director of research for marriage and family ministries. They are the authors of several books on family issues, including *The Family*.

Families in Pain

Working through the Hurts

Judith and Jack Balswick

Fleming H. Revell
A Division of Baker Book House Co
Grand Rapids, Michigan 49516

©1997 by Judith and Jack Balswick

Published by Fleming H. Revell
a division of Baker Book House Company
P.O. Box 6287, Grand Rapids, MI 49516-6287

Printed in the United States of America

Library of Congress Cataloging-in-Publication Data

Balswick, Judith K.
    Families in pain : working through the hurts / Judith and Jack Balswick.
        p.   cm.
    Includes bibliographical references (p.).
    ISBN 0-8007-5621-5 (pbk.)
        1. Family—Religious life. 2. Suffering. 3. Stress (Psychology)
    4. Problem families. 5. Suffering—Religious aspects—Christianity.
    6. Stress (Psychology)—Religious aspects—Christianity.
    7. Family—United States. I. Balswick, Jack O. II. Title.
    BV 4526.2.B356   1997
    248.8'6—dc21   96-46250

To
Jeff,
Frances,
Orville,
Arvid,
and
Todd

Contents

Part Four: Dealing with Traumatic Loss

Part Five: Step into the Future

Acknowledgments

Family pain powerfully impacts each of us and our families, and when left unattended, it continues to pass down from one generation to the next in even more painful scenarios. Many of our stories illustrate that we do not exist—feel, think, behave—in isolation from others. Jack and I are clearly indebted to the families that bravely shared with us their personal hurts, giving us all a deeper appreciation for how working through the hurts can lead to a healing peace. These families' stories of pain and hope brought life to this book.

Anita Maher brought so much of herself to this project, both as a sensitive therapist and as a family educator. Her research and knowledge are especially noteworthy in the areas of infertility, post-traumatic stress, violence, and therapeutic interventions for children and their families during such tragedies. It was also a great privilege to have Dave Wimbish add his creative touches to our book. Since both Anita and Dave are well acquainted with personal pain, they have gifted us with the wisdom that comes from a depth of understanding. Wendy Peterson and Brian Phipps took special care in the final editing of the manuscript, and William Petersen encouraged us from the beginning and along the way.

For those who are in the midst of tragic loss and suffering at this very moment, we pray that you will sense the gentle moving of God's love and feel the tender touch of God's Spirit. It's a holy journey you're on that can bring you nearer to God and to the community of God.

PART 1

When Life Comes Crashing In

1

Family: The Pain Starts Here

"We think your son has bone cancer."

The words tumbled out of the doctor's mouth in a dull monotone. He might as well have told us he thought it was going to rain.

We turned and looked at each other, both of us thinking, "Did he just say what I think he said?"

The doctor just kept talking, seemingly unaware of the pain and shock ripping through us.

"It's called Ewing's sarcoma," he said, thrusting a book at us. "This will give you some information about it."

That terrible moment happened nearly twenty years ago, but the memories are still strong and clear enough to send cold shivers racing through us. It seems like it happened only a month or two ago, and twenty years from now it will still seem that way. It is one of those memories that brings back all the old hurts and feelings, and it will not fade with time.

In the same way, neither one of us will ever forget the cold and unfeeling way the doctor delivered that heartbreaking news, as if he were afraid to show the least bit of emotion, as if to do so would somehow rob him of life and health. Nor will we forget the outpouring of concern from family and friends that let us know we were not alone, that others were standing with us in our time of desperate pain.

Jeff was only nine years old. He had been in perfect health up until the last few weeks. We had thought that, if anything, he had picked up some type of virus. Maybe he needed some antibiotics—an injection or two—and then surely he'd be fine. It couldn't be cancer. It just couldn't.

As we sat there, trying to deal with all the confusion and terror that clouded our minds, neither one of us could really believe what the doctor said. He had to be wrong. Jeff didn't have cancer. He wasn't going to die. This sort of thing just couldn't happen to us.

Slowly, over the following hours, days, and weeks, we had to come to grips with the terrible reality of the doctor's words. Jeff did indeed have cancer. And the prognosis was grim.

The next few months were, for the most part, torture. First, the denial. Then the desperate search for a miracle. And finally, the realization that Jeff was not going to make it—that we were going to have to let him go home to be with God.

Yes, we know all about pain.

Certainly we are not the only parents who have ever suffered through the loss of a child. But we also know from firsthand experience what an unbelievably painful experience such a loss can be—even for people who know that all lives are in God's hands, who rest secure in the promise that all things do work together for the good of those who love him.

Three Ways of Handling Family Pain

Death—whether of a child, a spouse, a parent, or a sibling—is one of the worst types of painful experiences that can attack the family; but it is not the only type. Family life is full of all sorts of pain. That's not to say that there is more pain than joy in family life, but pain is there nevertheless, and it can be handled in several ways.

1. You can deny it by pasting a happy smile on your face and pretending that everything's fine when it's not.
2. You can try to walk away from it, thinking it will go away if you ignore it.
3. You can learn how to deal with it in a godly, courageous way, strengthening yourself and your family in the process.

Obviously, the third response is the best one. It is a response born out of the recognition that pain can be a stimulus to personal and family growth. The family that works together to overcome or deal with the problems of life is sure to grow stronger and closer as the years go by.

Unfortunately, it's not always easy to know how to handle the stresses and pains of family life. Our desire in writing this book is to provide a chart to help you and your family navigate some of life's most difficult and turbulent waters. Before we move on, we want to tell you a little bit about who we are and why we've taken it upon ourselves to write this book.

First of all, this book is written by people who have been through it. It's only because we have experienced our share of deep pain that we feel qualified to help you learn how you can best deal with your own pain.

Second, this is a book written by trained family educators. We know what we are talking about from a professional perspective as well as a personal one. We have both spent years working in the field of family dynamics, and both of us are now serving as professors of marriage and family at Fuller Theological Seminary in Pasadena, California.

Third, this book is written from the perspective of two people who know that Christ is Lord of all, who are committed to living their lives in obedience to his lordship and filtering what we know about human relationships through the truth of God's Word.

One of the things we know is that not all family pain comes from disasters like the one we've described regarding our son, Jeff. Much of the pain that overtakes us simply arises out of the "usual" occurrences of day-to-day life.

For example, there is pain in the early days of a marriage, when two people are learning how to live together. There is pain for young people who are learning how to be parents for the first time. There is pain for parents and teenagers who are struggling as they learn how to adjust to the changes that are taking place in their family. There is pain for the middle-aged married couple who must make difficult decisions regarding aging parents.

Pain comes from dozens of situations and circumstances, and our hope is that this book will help you deal with any and all of these different types of pain. We don't know who you are or what you're going through, but we do know that help is available.

You may be in the midst of a family crisis that is so overwhelming you can't begin to imagine how you or those you love will ever be able to recover. Take heart! You can overcome. With God's help, you can exchange pain for peace. We are writing this book to let you know that, whatever you may be going through right now, life *can* be good again.

We are also writing to those who want to learn how to be more helpful to others who are in pain. Drawing on both biblical and secular wisdom, we will offer some basic principles of how to accept and overcome painful events that occur in families. We will apply these principles to a variety of situations—some in which pain is predictable, and others in which it comes on suddenly; some in which the pain can be easily cured, and others in which it must be endured for a lifetime; some in which the pain is relatively mild, and others in which it is quite severe.

In all of these situations, we will suggest practical and creative ways for family and friends to join together to cope with the stresses and crises that inevitably come into the lives of all who live on this fallen planet.

We want you to know that whatever you're going through, whatever you've been through, you can recover. With God's gracious help, you can find your way back to the "normal" world. You can live with the understanding that, in spite of all the difficulty life often holds, the ultimate reality is that God is able, somehow, to make all things work together for your good.

May God bless you as you read on.

2

People Who Need People

Almost every day the newspaper is full of heart-wrenching stories:

> A family on its way home from a wedding in another state is involved in a terrible traffic accident, and several children are killed.
> Another family loses everything when fire races through its house.
> A young single mother fights a terminal illness and wonders what will happen to her little ones when she is gone.

We shake our heads in sorrow when we read about such things. We may offer up a prayer on behalf of the ones who are suffering and perhaps even shed a few tears. But for most of us, underneath it all is the feeling that "something like that could never happen to me."

Then one day you get the shock of your life when you find out that yes, it *can* happen to you. Yes it *did* happen to you. What do you do? Where do you go?

For us, that shattering experience came the day we found out Jeff had cancer.

Jeff was a normal little boy. He loved baseball and bicycles, and he had his whole life in front of him. There was no way in the world this could really be happening. But it was.

You may be facing a similar reality. You may be grieving and in pain over the loss of an important relationship through divorce, separation, rejection, death, or even over something as normal as growing up or moving away. Perhaps you are in pain because you and your family are overwhelmed by the losses inherent in growing old, by the passing seasons of your lives, by failed expectations or economic hardships. Maybe your grief of today is compounded by the pain of your childhood—pain that has not yet been dealt with properly.

The pain you experience through any of these things may make you vulnerable and fragile in a number of ways, from the way you think to the way you feel and behave. Even your physical body may suffer when you're dealing with pain and grief, making you prone to colds and fatigue. When crisis hits, it can literally knock the breath right out of you. It can leave you reeling and incapable of properly dealing with the situation. (For a discussion of the various stages of grief, see appendix 2.)

When One Suffers, All Suffer

Whether you realize it or not, the problems that affect you also affect your family. In 1 Corinthians 12:26, Paul says that all believers are part of the body of Christ, so much so that "if one part suffers, every part suffers with it." That's an apt description of the way things work within the human family too.

When one member of the family or community suffers, all the other members share in and are affected by that pain. In fact, family pain is so powerful that, left unnoticed or unattended, it can become part of a family's heritage, passed down from one generation to the next.

Because an individual's pain is also a family's pain, it is vitally important to understand both the individual's and the family's response to stress so that the entire family can be better prepared to respond when a crisis occurs. That's why we're going to spend some time in the pages ahead talking specifically about stress.

Why is it that when one member of the family hurts all the members hurt? Because that's the way God designed us to live—within the context of community. Human beings operate at their optimum level when they are in proper relationships with other human beings. God built us in such a way that we need to support one another, to be empathetic, to share one another's burdens. So we do all these things—even though sometimes we may not really want to.

We just can't help it, because all human beings were created by God with an innate need to be involved in relationships. We can see this in God's declaration that "it is not good for man to be alone" (Gen. 2:18 NKJV). God was satisfied with creation only after Adam and Eve were together and experiencing true intimacy with each other and their Maker in the Garden of Eden.

When Adam and Eve sinned, they damaged humankind's communion not only with God (an alienation that brought death into the world), but with one another as well. Yet throughout Scripture it is quite clear that God's intention is to restore the relationships that have become estranged. In fact, concern for the pain of our alienation led God to send his only Son to suffer and die on our behalf. He made this sacrifice in order that the human family might be reconciled with their Creator God and with each other, and that we might, thereby, have life.

Our very lives are dependent on our being in a proper relationship with others. God created us to be in a relationship with him. Our salvation comes through being in a relationship with Jesus Christ. Our social, physical, emotional, and spiritual health depends on our relationships with other members of our family, and so on.

In God's grand scheme of things, the individual's health and identity are dependent to a great degree on his or her relationships. What Barbra Streisand sang so long ago is true—people *do* need people. What's more, the people you need most are those who belong to the meaningful and complex "system" that makes up your family. No one feels, thinks, or behaves in isolation. We are all affected to some degree by what is going on in the lives of other family members—how they are feeling, thinking, and behaving. And just as they affect us, we also affect them.

In other words, what we do and who we are is, in part, a reflection of who we are in relationship with others—primarily other members of the immediate family. At the same time, the thoughts, feelings, and behaviors of others in the family are affected, to some degree, by our own.

For example, you have probably noticed how your family's characteristics differ in many ways from those of your friends. That's because each human group—whether the smaller immediate family or the larger extended family—functions as a unit with its own distinct personality. We learn together, grow together, and are shaped by the experiences that affect us all.

This understanding of our basic nature helps us to better comprehend the emphasis God's Word places on community. It is here, in the groups that are most important to us, that we go about the business of caring for and supporting one another, of being cared for and supported. Romans 12:4–5 explains Christian community this way: "Just as each of us has one body with many members, and these members do not all have the same function, so in Christ we who are many form one body, and each member belongs to all the others."

Looking at life's hurts from the perspective of the entire family helps us seek out healing in a broader context of support. And by engaging in meaningful relationships with one another, healing on a deeper level can occur.

Who Is My Family?

A question we're often asked as we talk about dealing with family pain is, "What do you mean by 'family'?"

There is no clear-cut response to this question, especially in these closing days of the twentieth century, when most families are spread out all over the country and sometimes all over the globe. It is rare these days to have the entire extended family, grandmothers and grandfathers included, living in the same area. Many families keep in touch only through an occasional telephone call or perhaps even a fax. Add to this the fact that many families have been fractured and mixed together through divorce and remarriage.

No, it's not always easy to know exactly who fits into your family. But certainly your family includes you, your parents and siblings, and your spouse and your children. It may also include aunts, uncles, cousins, and grandparents. And it will include "adoptive kin"—people who aren't really related to you but who have become so close that you feel as if they are or wish they were.

We think of someone who recently moved from one part of the country to another. She was leaving behind a circle of close friends she had made during more than ten years of life in her adoptive community to return to the area where her parents and several other family members lived. She told us later that even though she was coming home to her family, she felt very much as if she were leaving her family behind. The people she knew in her new community had become her adoptive kin.

Such adopted relatives are especially important to those who do not have family readily available to support them. For that reason, throughout this book we will place special emphasis on deepening relationships with people outside of our immediate families.

Before we get down to the nitty-gritty of learning how to deal with family pain, you may want to take some time to chart your family's history of dealing with crises and stressful events. Such a chart can be a useful tool to help you understand how your family has shaped the way you think, feel, and react. Thus, it can help you learn how to deal with and change areas of your life that need special attention.

Using the diagram on page 24 as a guide, you can begin mapping out three generations of your family history, developing what is called a genogram. In drawing up this chart, you should trace the painful events that have occurred within your family—suicides, mental health problems, failures in business, alcoholism, deaths, divorces, whatever you can think of that has brought stress and pain into your family.

Draw circles around or lines between members to indicate how such problems have continued throughout the generations. You may want to use different colored pencils or pens to help you track the various threads that run through the generations of your family. For example, for all family members who have struggled with an addiction of some type, you may choose to color in the bottom third of their circle or square with a red marker. Broken lines may be drawn between family members whose relationships are strained or abusive. A bold line may signify relationships that are overly close or tangled together. And so on.

Sample Genogram: A Multigenerational Family Diagram

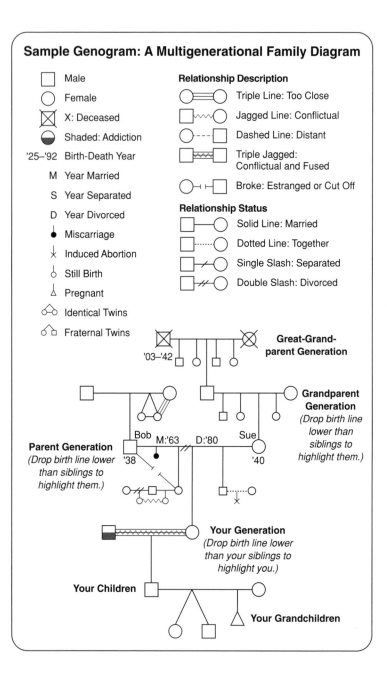

Male

Female

X: Deceased

Shaded: Addiction

'25–'92 Birth-Death Year

M Year Married

S Year Separated

D Year Divorced

Miscarriage

Induced Abortion

Still Birth

Pregnant

Identical Twins

Fraternal Twins

Relationship Description

Triple Line: Too Close

Jagged Line: Conflictual

Dashed Line: Distant

Triple Jagged: Conflictual and Fused

Broke: Estranged or Cut Off

Relationship Status

Solid Line: Married

Dotted Line: Together

Single Slash: Separated

Double Slash: Divorced

Great-Grand-parent Generation

'03–'42

Grandparent Generation
(Drop birth line lower than siblings to highlight them.)

Bob M:'63 D:'80 Sue

Parent Generation
(Drop birth line lower than siblings to highlight them.)

'38   '40

Your Generation
(Drop birth line lower than your siblings to highlight you.)

Your Children

Your Grandchildren

In drawing up your genogram, it's a good idea to talk to your parents or another close relative about events in the family that have been kept secret. Of course, make sure you explain carefully why you're doing what you're doing. The last thing you want is for the old rumor mill to start turning with questions about why you're interested in digging up all the family's old dirty laundry. It's important to help the other members of your family understand that your intent is positive—that it is precisely because you care about your family that you want to know about its struggles throughout the years.

Why is this type of investigation so important? Because shameful secrets can have a profound impact throughout the generations.

Judy remembers going to family reunions as a young girl and overhearing the older women whisper about her developmentally handicapped cousin. "Isn't it a shame?" "It's so hard on Jane." "It must be from her side of the family." All sorts of muffled messages revealed the family's deeply felt shame regarding this "different member."

She also remembers family members talking in hushed and shamed tones about an uncle who committed suicide. After a while they avoided the topic altogether. Of course they were hurt by his death, but they were also shamed by it. The feeling seemed to be that dealing openly with such an event would bring harm to the entire family. Actually, we think it's the other way around. It's the untold secrets, the buried skeletons, that can hurt the most.

Remember, though, that you're not just looking for the improper reactions to hard times and strained relationships. In drawing up your genogram, it's also important to recall events in which caring responses to crises were modeled. As an example of this, Judy remembers how, when she was twelve, her entire extended family gathered together to work on Uncle Bernie's farm after he was accidentally electrocuted. Every able-bodied person in the family worked extra hard that summer to take care of the seasonal crops so that Bernie's widow and children could survive the winter.

As you read this book, you may want to pull out your diagram from time to time to see what you have learned about the dynamics in your family. Add information as it becomes available. As you continue to explore the ways in which your family has managed stress, you'll begin to have a better understanding of your own responses. You'll also be able to identify strengths you wish to build on or hurtful patterns you wish to stop as you move into the future.

Responding to Another's Grief: Care That Empowers

When you've suffered through a time of devastating loss, it is difficult to get to the point where you're ready to move on and start building a future. It is easier if you have others around you who care enough to help you find the strength you need—people who know how to care for you without caretaking. There are significant differences between the two styles of relating:

> Caring brings empowerment.
> Caretaking often causes dependency.
> Caring says, "I want to help you move on."
> Caretaking says, "I'll do everything for you so you can stay tied to your grief and sorrow as long as you want to."
> Caring is often difficult.
> Caretaking is relatively easy.

Those who offer empowering care recognize the subtle difference between doing for others in a supportive way and doing for others what they are perfectly capable of doing for themselves. Unfortunately, it is easy to cross the line into caretaking, especially when people we love are hurting. It's natural, when we see their pain and frustration, to want to protect them, to make it all better, to spare them more agony. But a "take charge and do everything" effort actually ends up weakening and undermining the integrity of the individual who is suffering.

An empowerer believes that those who are in pain have a capacity and inner strength to find their way through it and that the best way to facilitate this process is to be there with a listening ear and a supportive shoulder. A caretaker believes that the person in pain cannot cope and so attempts to do everything for him or her.

Sometimes people cross from caring into caretaking because they cannot face their own pain. They can't bear to look too closely at what someone else is going through because, deep down, they are afraid of what that might stir up in them. When they move in to protect someone who is hurting, what they are really doing is protecting themselves. To give empowering care to others, we must be willing to share their pain and grieve our own unresolved losses, which may surface as a result of their situation.

Judy remembers clearly a particular incident in which friends demonstrated empowering care toward her. It happened when our son, Jeff, was being treated for cancer at the National Institute of Health in Bethesda, Maryland. Jack was already in Maryland, and Judy was driving by herself from Georgia to join them. Along the way, she was going to stop and spend the night with the McLelland family, friends of ours who lived in North Carolina.

She was doing fine until she reached the town where they lived. There, she lost her way and became so overwhelmed with anxiety that she feared she would never be able to find her way to their house. She ended up calling our friends and asking them in her most desperate-sounding voice to come and get her.

They said no. They weren't mean or rude about it. Rather, they assured her that she would be able to follow the directions they gave her over the phone.

That may not sound like much, but it was exactly what Judy needed. She needed to believe not only that she was capable of finding her way to their house but also that she was capable of making it the rest of the way to Maryland. Reassured by our friends' calmly expressed belief in her abilities, Judy gained strength and hope. When she did finally get to their house, the whole family greeted her with warmth and encouragement, with the result that she felt competent and strong rather than weak and helpless. All these years later, she remembers that single incident as a turning point that helped carry her through the difficult weeks that lay ahead.

Our friends knew how to give empowering care. They were not cold and distant, nor did they belittle Judy's pain and fear, but rather they encouraged her in a warm and loving way to do for herself what they knew she could do for herself. Then, when she reached their home, they did not brush her off with a shrug and a "things will work out" or a "God has it all under control" platitude. Instead, they listened with sensitivity as she openly shared her anguish and fears with them. They grieved with Judy, but they also comforted her with their love and faith, and where appropriate, they gave supportive advice.

The next morning, they surrounded her with prayer before she continued her journey. Judy remembers that she left their house with a renewed sense of hope that God would be her refuge in this time of trouble. This family's unfailing belief that God would see us through each difficult step of the way encouraged both of our hearts during the next few difficult months. They were a family of empowerers who made a great difference in our lives.

We end this chapter with a poem our daughter, Jacque, who was thirteen at the time, composed a few months after Jeff's death:

A Tear
A tear.
One solitary drop
filled with
overflowing emotion
revealing something deep
within the heart soul.

A symbol of love,
joy, fear, sorrow.
So simple, small,
Yet overpowering.
So uncomplicated
in this world of
confusion.

—Jacque Balswick

Learning
to Cope

Life Goes On was the name of a popular (and often very good) television show of a few years back. It was a show that struck a familiar chord with many of us as we watched the actors make their way week after week through some of life's difficult problems.

We all want to believe that we'll have the courage to "go on" when we have problems. We want to know that we won't "go under" when life gets rough, that we can summon the inner strength and courage to emerge victorious from life's school of hard knocks. But when one of those knocks is such a severe blow that it pushes your feet out from under you, it can be extremely difficult just to keep going, to get to the point where life truly does go on.

Judy remembers how, when Jeff was sick, she wanted the whole world to stop and pay attention to the agony that was unfolding in our lives. One day, when the checkout lady at the grocery store greeted her with a friendly, "How are you today?" she remembers that her first reaction was to shout out that she was absolutely terrible. She wanted everyone in that grocery store to know that our son had cancer and that things were hellish. Instead, she held her tongue, knowing that life was going on as usual for most of the people in that store, even though the Balswicks' world seemed to be crashing in all around us.

Many times both of us went through the motions of living, walking through the day-to-day tasks of life in a trance-like state. How were we supposed to keep going after doctors told us our precious son had only a few months to live? We were going to keep living, but our son was going to die. Faced with that terrible truth, the only thing we could do was to choose life—to make those last days together the best quality they could possibly be. But we couldn't have done this without the support of family and close friends. Eventually, as we came to terms with what had occurred, we began to grow stronger and wiser and to rediscover meaning and pleasure in life once again.

Whatever may be going on in your life right now, you, too, can find your way back to solid ground—especially if you are familiar with the tools family members can use to empower one another and ease the journey back to healthiness, wholeness, growth, and strength.

Much practical insight in this area has been offered by Reuben Hill, a social scientist who studied many families in times of stress. He discovered three important factors that determine how people cope with stress: *perception, resources,* and *vulnerability.* Let's take a close look at each of these factors to find out how they play a part in your family's ability to recover from stressful situations.

Perception

Perception is the way we look at what has happened to us, our beliefs about what happens to us or our family members, and the meaning we attach to stressful situations. To explain this further, let's take a look at the way three different families faced the same challenge of a father leaving home.

First, the Williams family. The father, Gary, was a military man who had been called overseas to fight for his country. For the most part, his leaving was perceived as a noble thing to do, but it was still a painful loss for his family. Major adjustments would be necessary, but because his wife and children perceived his leaving as honorable, they were more easily motivated to work hard at doing their part to adapt while Dad was away. His absence would be a hardship, but the family pulled together, knowing they had the support of the whole country.

In our second family, the father, Bill Clark, unexpectedly left without giving any explanation. Each member of the family had a unique interpretation of why this happened. Margaret wondered if it was because she just wasn't a good enough wife, while the children believed it was their misbehavior that chased Dad away. The personal and family pain of the desertion took a heavy emotional toll, leaving a number of unanswered questions and bad feelings in the hearts of those left behind. The family felt shamed by Bill's actions, and all were left with feelings of debilitating self-doubt. They also experienced feelings of anger, guilt, and resentment. Family members didn't know how they would manage their lives without Bill's assistance, and they felt victimized by an unjust situation. Their perceptions of the event ensured that they would have a difficult time adjusting to Bill's absence.

In the third family, Grant Hayes left because he had been mandated to enter an inpatient alcoholism treatment program after his third citation for driving while under the influence. Because his alcoholism had also made Grant verbally and physically abusive, the family felt they would be better off when he was gone, even though they were sad about his leaving. They would have adjustments to make, of course, but since Sharon Hayes and her kids viewed Grant's leaving as an opportunity for positive change, their capacity to cope would be stronger than the Clarks'.

As you can see, in each of these situations the perception of the painful loss influenced how the family coped with the stress triggered by the father's leaving. Healthy coping involves the use of what we call "empowering beliefs"—taking a wide enough view to see both the positive and negative aspects of every situation. It is vitally important that you don't become bogged down to the point of seeing only the negative or try to survive by minimizing the situation and lying to yourself about what is really happening. If you want to build an empowering belief structure, you must widen your perspective to the point where you can analyze as critically and thoroughly as possible the dilemma facing you.

Consider how Margaret Clark took the news that her husband was leaving. She believed that she was doomed, that life was hopeless, and that, therefore, she was helpless. Was she going through a bad time? Of course she was. So who can blame her for feeling as if the world was full of gloom and doom? And yet, she had to find a way to move beyond that. She would have been so much better off if she had at least tried for a while to take a look at some of the positives in her life, if she had believed in herself enough to think that she could somehow find a way to get through this difficult period. It would have helped her see that she was capable of surviving, that her life had meaning and purpose despite having been deserted by her husband.

A proper perception of whatever dilemma you may be facing can give you the energy to build on and use your resources, the second of three ingredients that determine your ability to cope.

Resources

As we all know from experience, a stressful event forces us to figure out a way to cope. A resource is anything you draw upon to help you cope. Resources may include your faith, personality traits, strong friendships, community ties, or any special training that may be used during a crisis. Obviously, the more resources a family has available to it, the better able it will be to cope with and manage a stressful situation.

In our first example, the Williams family was able to take advantage of both personal strengths and community resources in the absence of their husband and father. The wife, Caroline, was able to draw upon her internal resources of self-esteem and her employable skills to find meaningful work. Self-confidence and independence are some of the qualities in her children that contributed to the entire family's stability. The children were good students when Dad was home, and they continued to do well in their studies during his absence. Teachers served as resources as they attended to the Williams' children with special sensitivity. Extended family members also pitched in by taking time to visit, attending special events involving the kids, and allowing family members to share their emotions.

The Williams family also had a number of other resources that helped them through this difficult time: their church and community and government agencies, which provide special financial, medical, and educational aid to families of servicemen. All of these resources—personal, family, and community—provided physical and emotional support, thus empowering the family during its time of stress.

In the second scenario, the Clark family had a much more difficult time dealing with the situation. Since Margaret and the children were dependent on Bill, they found it difficult to cope with his desertion. Margaret was so devastated that she became clinically depressed, fearful, and seemingly helpless. In her weakened state, she leaned heavily on her children for help. Because they were struggling to handle their own fears, doubts, and pains, the added stress of trying to meet their mother's needs was almost more than they could bear. And because they lacked parental guidance and security, they acted out their angry impulses at school and soon were labeled "troubled" by their teachers. The Clarks were reluctant to call on church or community members for help because of their shame at being deserted. They felt they had nowhere to turn—as if all of society had turned away from them on the day Bill left.

To make matters worse, Margaret's paycheck was inadequate to meet the family's expenses, and her work performance was hindered by her depression. She was able to get aid through the local welfare office but felt degraded by the entire process. The Clarks' perception of the difficult situation, combined with the added injury caused by inadequate resources, spun this family into a hopeless downward spiral, with no knowledge of where to turn to find a way out.

Now let's consider the third family's resources. Grant Hayes' addiction had clearly affected the whole family in negative ways, so in this case, his absence gave his wife and children the opportunity to develop a better life without him. Sharon had worked herself into a managerial position during the last six years while Grant's drinking had kept him from holding down a regular job. Her job success, coupled with the self-understanding she had gained through her involvement with AL-ANON, had helped her build strong personal resources.

The children also had the resources they needed to handle the situation well. That all started with Mom, who instead of collapsing into a pool of self-pity and fear, worked hard to affirm the children and strove to teach them more independence and responsibility during their father's absence by giving them more of the household chores to do. With Dad gone, the kids were better able to focus on their schoolwork and their own personal goals, since the focus was no longer on Dad's destructive and unpredictable behavior. They were also involved in the ALATEEN program, which enabled them to meet new, supportive friends. The family crisis was the impetus for personal change and empowerment for the entire family. While Sharon and the children loved Grant, they knew they had to prepare themselves for a future with or without him. They did not allow themselves to be victimized by his irresponsible choices.

So far, we've seen that the way you perceive an event, coupled with your ability to tap into internal and external resources to support you, determines to a great degree your vulnerability during times of stress and crisis. Vulnerability, in fact, is the last factor that determines your (and your family's) coping ability.

Vulnerability

Have you been able to successfully navigate your way through a painful situation in the past? If so, you're less likely to feel helpless and vulnerable when a new challenge comes your way. The saying "Nothing succeeds like success" certainly applies here. Empowerment begets empowerment. If your family has a positive belief structure that can be carried into battle against any type of crisis, and if your family has available to it the resources necessary to overcome adversity, then it is likely to be able to adapt—and carry on in an effective manner—when the winds of crisis start blowing.

On the other hand, if past family crises were merely "survived," with only minimal attention given to how everyone was individually and collectively affected by the event, then you're going to have less strength and skill at your disposal the next time life throws you a punch.

So the more your family has successfully braved crises in the past, the less vulnerable you will be in the future.

Vulnerability is also linked to the stability of your family environment. If your family provides a safe and nurturing atmosphere, then parents and children alike will have the structure and stability needed for creative change to take place. To be more specific, certain distinct family relationship patterns promote stability, while others lead to increased vulnerability.

Promoters of Stability

Connectedness. Families handle pain best when there is a balanced degree of interpersonal connectedness. A family has achieved a proper connectedness when there is a good balance between togetherness and independence. Overly dependent family members have a way of dragging each other down in a crisis, whereas a family in which the members do not relate well to each other will not have the emotional support and teamwork needed to overcome duress.

In the Clark family, for example, we saw Margaret compounding the family's difficulties by her dependence on her children. Meanwhile, lacking parental modeling, the children did not know how to communicate their needs and feelings with their mother or each other, so they ended up acting out their hurt in unfortunate ways.

Good family connectedness occurs when members of a family can share deeply both their joys and sorrows with one another yet also respect one another's limits and differences. In such a family there is a sense of give-and-take, a mutuality in which there is nonintrusive caring and support for one another. Family members know how to trust each other, and they do not violate or take advantage of another's trust. The support that is offered empowers, therefore, instead of promoting dependence. Both the Williams and Hayes families model good interpersonal connectedness. The Williams family was able to work together as a team, united in their love and support of one another. The same was true in the Hayes family. Sharon offered her alcoholic husband empowering care, letting him know that the family loved him and wanted him to be a healthy part of their lives, but that she would not let herself or the children suffer as the result of his destructive behavior. She tended to her emotional needs by seeking out other adults, not her children, for support. Thus, she remained the "adult parent," which allowed her to respond to the needs of her children. By involving the children in ALATEEN, she respected their need to sort some things out in private with other caring adults and peers. By involving them in household chores, she empowered her children, rather than crippling them through indulgence based on pity.

Adaptability. Adaptability means organizing family life to promote the structure and security necessary for growth. Family life is never static; it is always changing. Adaptability relates to whether a family is willing to change its way of doing things as the needs of individual members dictate. It involves how family roles and rules are defined, how it is determined who does what in the family, and how all of that is communicated. If a family's structure is too rigid, then family members can't bend and sway in the wind when a storm blows up. The entire family is in danger of cracking under pressure. If, on the other hand, a family has little or no structure, then stress is likely to make life more chaotic, and the family may fragment and blow apart when crisis hits. Adaptability is the quality that helps you make the crucial adjustments that every crisis demands.

All families go through change. Children are born. Children grow up. Parents age. A job transfer means a move to a new community. And so on. Families that are adaptable to these sorts of changes will have a head start when it comes to coping with extreme stress.

During times of stress it may be necessary for some members of the family to shift responsibilities or roles in the family. This may be temporary or permanent. It is adaptability that allows this to happen and keeps the family functioning as smoothly as possible.

For example, when the father leaves the home, a vacuum is created that must be filled. If the father's role is rigidly defined, no one in the family will feel able to fill the gap, and then the loss will take an even more devastating toll on everyone else. Mom may resent taking on a full-time job, believing that she shouldn't have to do so. Or since she never prepared herself for employment outside the home, her choices may be extremely limited. There may even be loyalty issues that prevent family members from expanding their roles to take up the slack. For instance, some people may feel as though the family is trying to prove that Dad wasn't all that important anyway. Finding that offensive, they resist changes that need to be made.

In our examples, the Williams and Hayes families were both able to adapt to carry on without Dad. In fact, the new responsibilities the two mothers and their children took on resulted in the development of stronger character and increased competency.

In the Clark family, however, everyone depended on Dad to an extreme, which, as it turned out, was one of the reasons he left. He just couldn't take the burden anymore, even though it was largely a burden he had brought upon himself. When he left, the family collapsed without him. What Bill should have done when the pressure first started to get to him was sit down with his wife and family and figure out how to make some changes to improve things for him—and probably for everybody else in the family too. Instead, he chickened out and ran away. He couldn't adapt while he was still at home, and his wife and children couldn't adapt after he left. The result was that the entire family crashed in on themselves in a suffocating way, making it more and more unlikely that they could ever get beyond their problems.

Promoter of Vulnerability

Pileup. You know the old saying "When it rains, it pours." When you're late for work, you not only can't find your shoes but the keys seem to disappear too. Meanwhile, the kids seem to be in "mule mode," and nothing you offer them for breakfast seems appealing. Then, to top it off, when you finally do get in the car and on your way, you only get about a block before the tire goes flat.

We've all had days that went pretty much like that. The term piled-up vulnerability simply refers to those times when we're attacked by a series of crises that hit too close together. We are left reeling and unable to cope with the demands of everyday life, let alone the aftermath of the latest few crises. When any individual is hit with wave after wave of crises, he or she is going to be more vulnerable and less able to cope with each successive blow. When your reserves are depleted, you simply cannot cope.

The amount of change that is necessary also influences how well we cope with a crisis. When the family experiences only a small amount of change due to a stressful event, such as a noninjurious car accident, we are usually able to adjust our daily routines, find the necessary resources, and cope effectively. However, if the stressor event requires a great amount of change in the daily routine or if the family has an accumulation of pain, we become more vulnerable.

Bill Clark's desertion of Margaret and their children is a good example of a family experiencing piled-up vulnerability. Stress existed in this marriage prior to Bill's leaving, but neither he nor Margaret tended to the signals. Instead, the stress continued to build and eat away at the family's coping energy. Bill's abandonment alone was enough to cause piled-up vulnerability for Margaret, but then there was the additional crisis of figuring out how to provide for her family as a single mother. Perhaps the most significant victims in the entire situation were the children. Their stress levels were being taxed right along with their parents prior to their father's leaving. And then, when he did leave and life took an extreme turn toward chaos, this piled-up vulnerability began to take its toll as the children started to withdraw and behave aggressively with each other and with their peers.

To Whom Do We Turn?

As we've seen, a family's ability to cope is largely dependent on its perceptions, resources, and vulnerabilities. In all of this, it should be apparent that recovery from stressful situations is aided by healthy relationships. When you have people in your life who care about you, it's easier to deal with difficult situations. These caring people may be members of the family or close friends. During painful times, most people look first to other members of the immediate family for support, then to members of the extended family, and, finally, to friends.

It would be difficult to overestimate the importance of good friends. In some ways, a good friend may be able to help more in a time of crisis than another member of the family. This is true primarily because a friend is often able to see things from a completely different perspective, since he or she is not directly tied in to the emotional pain affecting the family. A friend may be able to offer advice or make excellent suggestions that would be overlooked by other family members, simply because they are too close to the situation.

Friends can also care for you with a depth and sincerity you didn't experience at home. We refer to such friends as adoptive kin. If you are distanced in some way from the other members of your family—whether geographically or emotionally—you especially need to have friends who will be there for you when life hurts.

In counseling people who are dealing with family pain, we have come to see clearly the important role of these adoptive kin. As an example of how important these people can be, consider the christening and child dedication ceremonies that take place in many of our churches. As the parents and godparents pledge to nurture and love the child, the entire community of believers is also asked to pledge its support. This is a pledge based on the knowledge that our families do not grow up strong and healthy in isolation but in community with other caring people.

Whom do you consider to be a part of your community? Whom do you—or could you—turn to when you are in pain? Do you allow family and friends to care for you? Is it okay for friends to turn to you for comfort and aid?

Yes, friends are vitally important. And, as we're about to see, so is faith.

4

Hanging On to Faith in Times of Trouble

Twelve years ago, Sean and Karen were a newly married couple that faced the future with anticipation and excitement. As far as they could see, there was nothing but blue skies and smooth sailing ahead. It was going to be great! But, boy, were they wrong!

Having grown up in good Christian homes, they both had a solid faith in Christ. They enjoyed praying and studying the Bible together and were active in their church, in which they served as youth leaders. They both believed that if they were faithful to God, he would supply their every need, protecting and guiding them as they went through life.

But then, three years into their marriage, a baby daughter was born. The couple's joy quickly turned to sorrow when they discovered that newborn Michelle was severely disabled and would require around-the-clock care. The grief they felt was not so much for themselves but rather for the pain their daughter would face growing up in a world that puts such a high premium on physical perfection. Still, they decided to leave the situation in God's hands, trusting that he would grant them all the grace they needed to deal with the painful situation.

And then, through no fault of his own, Sean was laid off from work. It didn't take him too long to find another job, but then he was laid off again. And again. He was a good worker, but due to one unusual circumstance after another, he could not keep a job. After the fifth layoff, he began doubting his faith and his worth as a husband and a father, and he felt like a failure as a man. Here he had been faithful all his life, and look where it had got him. He couldn't provide for his disabled daughter and his wife because he couldn't keep a job. Every Sunday at church he'd see other happy couples with two or three beautiful (and normal) children. There they'd sit, all dressed in their Sunday best, looking as if they didn't have a care in the world. He didn't like those feelings of jealousy, often bordering on rage, that stirred within him; but, really, who could blame him for feeling that way? What in the world was he doing wrong? He felt ashamed and worthless.

He was afraid to admit it to anyone—even to himself— but after eight years of continuous struggling, Sean had come to wonder if the God he had always trusted and loved was really nothing more than a hoax. After all, everywhere he looked he saw people who never thought about God sailing through life seemingly without a care in the world—driving fancy cars, living in palatial houses, and building up fat bank accounts. He couldn't help but wonder if his faith had really been based on nothing more than a big lie.

Have you ever felt that way? Perhaps not to the same degree—but have you ever wondered why bad things happen to people who are trying so hard to live for God?

If so, you're not alone. Just read through the Psalms and you'll find many examples of such doubt and anger directed at God. In Psalm 10, David expresses anger over

Yahweh's apparent passivity when the wicked prosper. In Psalm 79, Asaph accuses God of carrying wrath a bit too far. Psalm 88 is one long, despairing complaint. And in portions of Psalm 44, God is accused of turning over his people like sheep for slaughter. If you are sometimes confused by the apparent contradiction between the cruelties of life and the loving nature of God, you can at least find some comfort in knowing that the psalmists often felt the same way.

And yet, God is there and he does care.

God Responds to Our Pain

Although the psalmists obviously passed through times of anger and despair, they always came back to a belief in God's transcendent love and power. Many other biblical narratives also tell of men and women who were able to make their way through overwhelming difficulty to discover meaning and hope in life.

Paradise was lost when Adam and Eve disobeyed God. They not only lost their beautiful and secure home in the Garden of Eden but were also alienated from God and from each other. The situation was worsened when they refused to take responsibility for what they had done. Instead, Eve blamed the serpent, and Adam blamed Eve. They hid from themselves, from each other, and from God. Everything was lost! This shameful predicament brought about self-deception and the first great cover-up in history. Rather than face themselves and their crisis in a proactive way, they dug themselves deeper and deeper into trouble. And yet, even though Paradise was lost, a merciful God provided a way of healing. Although Adam and Eve's choices caused a deep and permanent rift in their relationships with God and with each other, God did not abandon them.

Noah's adventure is a story of hope in the midst of devastation. The whole family obeyed the commands of God against all rational odds, even though their ark-building project undoubtedly made them the butt of many cruel remarks and jokes from their neighbors. Then, as the rain poured down, and as they waited in the darkness of the ark, the world as they had known it came to an end. Noah and his family endured the agony of knowing that all other people on the earth had been destroyed. They endured long days and nights of uncertainty as the ark bounced about atop the waves. Yet, in the midst of all that, they held fast to God's promises. A bright hope finally came in the form of a dove, and then in a rainbow, a symbol of God's covenant love and power.

Abraham and Sarah certainly suffered when God asked them to sacrifice their only son, Isaac. Could it possibly be true that this child of miraculous conception and birth was to die by his father's own hand? It was only when God provided a substitute sacrifice at the last possible moment that they came to understand the full meaning of the covenant with Abraham—and what that covenant would mean to the generations yet to be born.

Then there is our old friend Job, whose story teaches us an important lesson about the persistent search for meaning in the midst of profound suffering and loss. He lost his children, his health, his reputation, and his wealth. He even lost his wife and friends, who tried to convince him that his troubles were the result of his own sin. His entire support system collapsed. He had lived a righteous life, and the circumstances that befell him were undeserved and unfair. And yet, despite his anger, frustration, and doubt, he refused to give in to the haunting thought that his suffering was without meaning or purpose. He persevered in asking God to respond to his plight and continued on when the pain was beyond what most human beings could endure. He kept calling out to God even when there was no reply.

Many of Job's myths and misperceptions about God were challenged as he passed through his trials:

> He learned that good and righteous people are just as vulnerable and susceptible to troubles as anyone else.
> He learned that God can handle our anger and confusion.
> He learned that we may never fully understand why unjust things happen to us.

But he also learned that, despite the trials we may suffer, our God is an all-powerful, all-knowing Being who does not abandon us, who loves us even though we may not understand why life is so difficult. In his suffering, Job found the deeper meaning of life.

Throughout the entire Old Testament, we often see God imparting love and grace amid some harsh circumstances. It's easy to become confused about God's nature, especially when it appears as though some people are protected by his might while others are left vulnerable to everything the evil forces of the universe can throw at them. We have to search hard to understand God's nature through the lives and culture of another time.

The New Testament gives us a clearer glimpse of God's response to our pain. It is there that we see how God, moved with love and compassion for our suffering and the pain of our separation from him and from one another, sent his only Son to us. Jesus became flesh and blood and then took upon himself the suffering of the world. He suffered and died to give us hope and comfort today and to guarantee that someday there will be an end to all suffering.

In taking upon himself the form of a human being, the Son of God became a suffering servant. He was ridiculed, falsely judged, tempted, misunderstood, driven out of his own city, denied, rejected, tortured, humiliated, and finally, crucified.

As he approached his death, Jesus was in such mental and emotional agony that he sweat drops of blood while praying for some other way to redeem humankind. As Jesus cries out from the cross, "My God, my God, why have you forsaken me?" we see the Son of God fully joined with us in the human experience of alienation from God. As the Just One Who Suffers, Jesus not only died for the sins that separate us from God but also experienced the forsakenness we feel when we suffer.

Jesus knew that God would not keep him from suffering and death; but he had faith that God would keep him even in the midst of suffering and death, with his resurrection to be the ultimate proof of God's faithfulness.

But Why, Lord, Why?

We can see clearly from Scripture that God is compassionate, that his heart goes out to us when we suffer. Still, the question remains: Why do people suffer?

There are many reasons. We might be tempted to believe that God strikes us with infirmities to punish, teach, or strengthen us. Actually, the cause of our pain most often has a distinctly human origin. Sometimes it comes as the result of our own carelessness or immaturity. At other times it is simply because we are "merely human," subject to the mistakes and frailties of all finite creatures. Sometimes suffering comes because we live in a fallen world in which we inflict pain on one another. Whether we want to admit it or not, much of the suffering we endure is no one's fault—there's no one to blame.

Often, our suffering is meaningless in and of itself. There is no redeeming quality—not now, not ever. These are not incidents God has given to move us toward the completion of his purpose for us. They are occurrences in which no sense can be made of the event itself, occurrences that anger and grieve God.

Rather than inflicting pain on us, the God of the Bible is the One who comes alongside us in response to our suffering. It is often in the midst of the worst sort of pain that we sense God's presence in a stronger, deeper way. It is in God's response to our suffering that we can find ultimate meaning and purpose through the tragedies we endure. Through Jesus' life, death, and resurrection, evil is overcome, and God offers us compassion, empathy, and hope—including hope for justice to come—that can sustain us through this life. It is only when we sense that God is there, grieving with us, that we are able to give these events purpose and find deeper meaning in our pain.

When you are trying to recover from the pains of family life, it is natural to go through a season of questioning God, but it's important not to stop there. It's easy to become stuck on questions like, Why does God just stand by and let suffering happen? As the old hymn *Farther Along* says, "Farther along we'll know all about it, Farther along we'll understand why." But this side of heaven, there are no satisfactory answers to questions like that one. It's important to strive to leave those unanswerable questions behind and open your heart and mind to God's ultimate response to the dilemma of human suffering.

When Jesus healed the blind man, his disciples wanted to know why the man had never been able to see. They asked the Lord if the man was blind because of some sin that either he or his parents had committed. But by his answer Jesus firmly and simply showed them they were asking the wrong question. Jesus never saw a need to explain why suffering exists. He simply responded to the needs of those who were in pain (see John 9:1–3).

The answer to suffering for Jesus was the same as it ought to be for his followers today. The question is not, Why is there suffering? but, What are we going to do about suffering? It is a given that life is full of pain, so how are we going to respond to that pain? How are we going to be Christ's presence to those who suffer?

As we suggested earlier, if we are to be like Christ, we must all be willing to share in one another's suffering and do what we can to impart life and hope through our caring presence. There is great strength in standing together in the uncertainties of life. People who stand with you can help you grasp the truth of God's love and care, and you can do the same for people in pain as you stand with them. When we face crises together as God's people, we all find the mystery of God's grace.

So often, God demonstrates his love through the actions of others. For example, when Margery's father died, she brought her mother to visit her in California. A month later, when the time came for Mom to fly back home, Margery was nearly overcome with anguish. How would her mother be able to cope all by herself? Who would look out for her? She would be so terribly lonely! Her worry about her mother was compounded by guilt. She felt as if she were abandoning her mom.

But then, as they were waiting in the terminal for the boarding announcement, a fellow traveler struck up a friendly conversation with the two women. Then, as the boarding call came, Margery watched as this stranger helped her mother up the airplane stairs. At that moment she felt relief flood over her. She knew that God was caring for her mother through the kind action of a stranger and that the Lord was also relieving her own stress and anxiety about the situation.

As we've said before, people need people, and it is the community of friends, family, and neighbors that can make real for us the love and grace of God.

When our son was sick, we were amazed at the variety of ways people gave to us. Kay came by each week with special food she thought Jeff might like and sat with him while we had our supper in the other room. Nine-year-old Kathy had a magician come to the house to perform a magic show for Jeff, some of his friends from the neighborhood, and our family. Some of the University of Georgia football players brought Jeff an autographed football. Pastor Dan wrote special letters to Jeff. They were signed by his dog, Gumby, and they brought laughter and humor into our family when we needed desperately to find *anything* to smile about.

Dale drew pictures and made up stories about the adventures of Beeshaloppy and Ferkalmonia to help Jeff and Jacque deal with the reality of cancer. Our neighbor, Leis, brought in an entire tank of exotic fish to sit at the foot of Jeff's bed. Jeff's pediatrician and her office staff of nurses came to our house to attend to his medical needs so he could stay home the last two months of his life. Our church prayed faithfully each week and ministered to us through special gestures of love.

It would have been so awful to be without the loving support of such friends and family. What if we had been left alone to deal with our misery? Mere survival would have been a terrible struggle for all of us.

The compassion and nearness of friends brings meaning in the midst of painful experiences because it gives a profound sense that God "is close to the brokenhearted and saves those who are crushed in spirit" (Ps. 34:18).

Standing Together in a Circle of Vulnerability

Before moving on to discuss some of the specific challenges of family life, we want to leave you with one simple truth: God is present with you in every moment of pain or crisis.

This is true whether you sense it or not. And because it is true, you can know that in your vulnerability as a family, God is your ultimate security. He is the One who can give you vision, calm your fears, supply a proper perspective, and ultimately, guide you to the promised land of peace.

God is right in the middle of your pain. When we all stand together in suffering, confusion, and frailty, it is Christ who lights the way through the darkness. Thus, the journey through pain becomes a holy adventure. You will be transformed as you hold on to God when you hurt. Jesus knows what you need and wants to take part in your healing.

But before healing can come, you must seek the One who has the power to heal your wounds. Like the invalid mentioned in the fifth chapter of John, you must do your part to regain wholeness. You must immerse yourself in the healing pool of God's love. And when you do this, a miracle will happen. The darkness will lift, and you will be able to see, as if for the first time in your life. You will be empowered. And you will be able to gratefully acknowledge the One who has performed the healing miracle.

It is Christ, the only begotten of the Father, who has unveiled the darkness that we all might live in the true light.

Time for Reflection

1. Take a few moments to reflect on the stressful event(s) taking place in your family right now. Are you trying to handle things all by yourself? If so, make a list

of the resources that are available to you to help you deal with the difficult situation.

2. In times of pain it may be helpful to write up a list of people who care about you—those relatives and friends God has brought into your life who are willing to share your pain and support you however they can. Think about how these people confirm God's love, care, and concern for you.

3. We have shared some stories from the Bible in which people experienced God's blessing in the midst of their pain. What other Bible stories have spoken to you regarding God's presence in times of trouble? Have you experienced God's presence in your time of difficulty?

4. Do you think it's okay to let God know you are confused or angry? How do you think he will respond to your frustrations?

5. Does it help you to know that Jesus shares in your suffering? How do you respond to the call to be his presence to people in pain?

PART 2

The Challenges of Family Life

5

The Fairy Tale versus Reality

There is a land where every family is a happy family. It is a land where the sun always shines, where problems—if they come at all—are tiny ones, easily solvable via a few words of wisdom from Dad or Mom. It is a land where all the girls are pretty, the boys handsome, all children are well behaved, and the parents are wise—a land of peace, harmony, and joy.

Unfortunately, that wonderful land exists only on television, in the happy world of the situation comedy. And even more unfortunately, Sitcom Land bears little resemblance to real life.

If you measure your own family by what you see on television—especially old television shows such as *Father Knows Best* or *The Cosby Show*—you're probably going to feel frustrated and disappointed by what goes on in your own house. The truth is that real family life can be painful. Problems are often big ones that can't be tied into neat little packages in a matter of thirty minutes. People can get on each other's nerves. Bad things can and often do happen.

But it doesn't take bad things to bring pain into a family's life. Instead, that pain may merely be the result of a family's growth, in much the same way as young children experience growing pains. You see, any family is constantly growing and changing. Children grow up, they marry, they move away from the nest, parents grow old, everybody changes in various other ways.

As a family passes through the various stages of its life together, there can be great joy, and there can be great pain. Family members may grieve for what has passed, struggle and groan through the tasks of the present, and even look with sadness and dread toward the future. Most of the time, family pain is due to the adjustments family members must make as they make the transition from one stage of family life to another.

Consider everyday events, such as the birth of a child, the day your teenager leaves home, or the time your elderly parent is no longer able to drive or care for himself or herself. In each case, these events affect the entire family because things will never be the same. Even in events that bring gain, such as marriage, there is also loss. And just as the amount of joy experienced through any given event will vary depending on a number of factors, so will the amount of pain.

In this section, we will focus on the usual and unusual stressors that can accompany the typical stages of family life. We will give special attention to the in-between times, referred to as family transitions, because they are the most disconcerting to family members—those times when major adjustments are necessary. Most important, we will talk about how a family can respond to the challenges of life in ways that promote growth, healing, and empowerment for all concerned.

How to Make Your Family Stronger

Those who have closely studied family stress have found that some families are better at coping than others. From the findings of those researchers, we have drawn six specific principles that help make families stronger.[1] As you read through these six factors, you may ask yourself, How is this going to help me now? My family already doesn't fit into this picture of "optimum growing conditions"! But even if you are getting this information "too late," it can still help you in a number of ways.

First, it can give you a greater understanding of what your family may be experiencing at this moment. This knowledge then allows you to make better-informed choices. It can help you just to know there's a reason behind your family's difficult circumstances. Such knowledge can enable you to take a breath and collect your thoughts so you can work through your crises with renewed energy and direction.

Second, family growth and maturation are ongoing processes. The coping and adjustment principles listed below can help you alter the course of things so your family will be stronger when the next crisis hits.

As you read about these six principles, consider how they apply to your family. In what ways is your family prepared for the impact of developmental stressors—of growing pains? In what ways is your family vulnerable? Think about what you could do to get your family to alter its course to better respond to what you are facing and to prepare for what life has in store for the family in the future.

Principle 1

Family life will be less stressful when family members master their own personal developmental tasks in a systematic fashion.

As your family passes through various stages of its life together, all of its members will constantly need to learn how to master certain psychosocial tasks. For example, learning how to trust others and ourselves gives us the necessary skills to tackle the more complex task of establishing intimate relationships. Problems arise when skills are not adequately developed for one area of life, because it is usually true that the next set of skills needed will build on the previous ones.

It's like learning math. If you learn the simple rules of addition, subtraction, multiplication, division, and so on, you can eventually move on to algebra and geometry. From there, trigonometry and calculus can be mastered. But if you never learn the basics of arithmetic, then it will be impossible for you to move on into areas of higher math. In the same way, if earlier developmental tasks are glossed over, you will be more likely to encounter challenges you are not prepared to handle. And that means, of course, that the stress of these new challenges will be much more intense and potentially overwhelming than you would otherwise expect.

This first principle notes that as each individual family member is growing and developing through his or her predictable, age-appropriate, individual life-cycle tasks, the family as a whole will be under less stress. This is not to say that individual developmental struggles won't cause some stress within the family, but that stress will tend to be minimized and more manageable.

Many models highlight different aspects of individual development, but we feel that one of the best is Erik Erikson's eight major stages of individual development.[2] Erikson reminds us that individual development does not occur in a vacuum. Children grow properly only as the result of being in dependable, caring, and loving relationships with parents and significant others.

We briefly describe those stages below, but for an in-depth look at what each stage involves and how we as parents can respond, we recommend Clarke and Dawson's parenting book, *Growing Up Again: Parenting Ourselves, Parenting Our Children.*[3] As you read our description of these various stages, keep in mind that people develop at different rates. And it is also true that males and females may master different skills at different times. For instance, females may be quicker when it comes to developing intimacy skills, whereas males may master identity questions at an earlier age.

- *Learning trust.* From the first year of life, a child's first and most important task is learning to trust. Accomplishing this task provides the foundation upon which all else is built.
- *Developing autonomy.* During the next several years, which encompass the "terrific twos," the child's task is to separate from his or her parents and discover his or her own individuality without fear.
- *The initiative stage.* Roughly between the ages of four and six, children are actively initiating new goals and challenges. Negative or inappropriate responses by parents will encourage the child to feel both incompetent and guilty for his or her efforts. Guilt leads to inhibition, which may lead the child to become overly dependent on others. When caretakers encourage their children to take initiative, those children will feel competent to master the tasks that are appropriate at this age.
- *The industry stage.* Between the ages of seven and twelve, children have much energy and curiosity, and enjoy tackling new tasks. With support from others, they eagerly take on challenges to do things for themselves, which leads to feelings of self-mastery. When children repeatedly fail—whether at

school, with peers, or in their parents' eyes—it leads to feelings of inferiority.

Jack enjoys taking our grandchildren skiing. Starting out on the easier slopes where they receive gentle instruction and encouragement from their grandfather, they glow with confidence as they tackle—and master—the initial challenges. Then, as their self-confidence grows, they eagerly move on to the advanced beginner and intermediate slopes. Jack presents our young family members with tasks that are age-appropriate, challenging, fun, and "doable," and he also walks by their sides, instructing and encouraging them in a highly personal and caring manner.

Initially, they believe in their ability to tackle the challenge because of their grandfather's belief in them. But then, with each success, they prove to themselves that they are, in fact, capable and competent. So they tackle the later challenges because they come to believe in themselves.

- *The stage of identity.* The major developmental task for children during the teen years is finding out who they are. If positive groundwork has been laid during the previous four stages of development, the teenager is likely to develop an integrated sense of who he or she is as an individual—connected to, yet separate from, parents, family, and friends. Failure to master the task of identity results in role confusion for the adolescent.

- *The stage of intimacy.* During young adulthood—between the ages of twenty and twenty-nine—people are mastering intimacy skills by learning what it means to be in close and lasting relationships with friends of the same and opposite gender. It is a time to discover differences and build tolerance for those who are different. The challenge here is to establish interdependent bonds with others. An inability to establish bonds with others outside of one's immediate family leads to feelings of isolation. Conversely, overinvolvement in intimate relationships with others signifies a losing of one's sense of self.

- *The stage of generativity.* The middle adulthood years (roughly between the ages of thirty and fifty) present the opportunity for generativity—bearing and raising children, being productive and creative in one's work, investing oneself in the lives of others. Stagnation is the opposite extreme of generativity.

- *The stage of ego integrity.* From age fifty and beyond, an individual should be learning to integrate the many parts of his or her life and self. Ego integrity is present when one has a sense of "centeredness," meaning, purpose, and fulfillment in the whole of one's life. The absence of ego integrity results in despair. If one's life is viewed as having been futile or unfulfilling, then anger, resentment, or bitterness may predominate.

Principle 2

Family life will be less stressful when the family as a whole has mastered the specific family tasks expected at that particular life stage.

Within each family life-cycle stage, our families face particular challenges that often produce some normal stress. The newlywed must learn how to set up a new household with his or her spouse; new parents must learn how to adjust to the ever-present needs of an infant; parents of older children must learn how to let go of their adult children and adjust to life as a couple again, and so on. This second principle reminds us that if we face the challenges of each stage of family life as they arise instead of trying to put them off, then the family's growth will continue in a healthy manner. By tending to the tasks at hand, normal stress is less likely to turn into debilitating stress. Completion of a task now means that the family will not have to play catch-up later on.

Admittedly, a number of situations can arise to prevent tasks from being completed on schedule—death of a family member, for example, or divorce. As we mentioned before, not all family members can expect to develop at the same pace or to meet the various tasks with the same degree of ease. But at the same time, the family is much better able to cope with the stress and strain of normal life when certain life skills and stages are accomplished in a timely and appropriate fashion.

On the other hand, if the family is stifled in its progress along the route to overall maturity, a pile-up occurs. When this happens, there are so many tasks to be accomplished in a short period of time that it becomes burdensome to everyone involved. Like water piling up behind the floodgates of a dam, so there will come a time when the accumulated force of that water causes the dam to burst.

Families who are able to deal appropriately with one task at a time, rather than having to deal with many tasks all at once, are better able to manage the daily stresses of family life.

For example, when a married couple experiences severe discord, the family unit itself fractures. The stability that Mom and Dad offer to their young children is shattered, even if the problems are only temporary. Home is no longer the safe haven a child needs to progress through his or her own developmental milestones. Meanwhile, the parents are having difficulty mastering the adult tasks of maintaining their relationship.

Sadly, it's often true that married couples begin experiencing trouble in their relationship just when their children need them most. Parents battle each other just when the children most need to feel secure and to know that Mom and Dad love each other *and* them. When this happens, every family member feels stress because the family is unable to function as a proper unit. In this state, the entire family is likely to have greater difficulty tending to the normal developmental challenges of its life together.

Principle 3

Family life will be less stressful when both the family and individual family members are on time in their developmental process.

Our first principle illustrated the importance of tending to our own maturation process. The second principle emphasized the importance of the whole family embracing and handling each task as it comes along, rather than putting it off. This third principle emphasizes being "on time," which refers to the importance of encountering life-cycle tasks within the normal age range—neither too early nor too late.

When a couple enters marriage for the first time at age forty and have their first child when they are forty-two, they are going through these family life stages later than most people. As a result of being out of sync with their peers, the possibility exists for additional stress. It may be hard to fit in to the peer group, since most people who are in their forties have older children and are no longer coping with problems like teething, colic, and ear infections. Therefore, the older couple with young children is likely to feel excluded and perhaps even ostracized. Support from the extended family may also be less available due to grandparents' increasing age. Or this couple may find that it is difficult giving up a lifestyle to which they have become accustomed.

A word of caution is necessary here: Do not assume that delayed entry into marriage, parenthood, or a career signifies dysfunction. There is a growing trend in America to start families later in life. This forty-something couple may find that they are more confident as parents and secure as providers than they would have been if they had started their family ten or fifteen years earlier. They have had time for individual pursuits and may be less likely to resent the changes in lifestyle that parenting makes necessary. Simply be aware that as each stage carries with it inherent stressors, we face the possibility of those stressors being intensified when they are encountered outside of what is normal in our culture.

This added stress was eloquently described to us by Elaine, a thirty-eight-year-old engaged woman who began expressing ambivalence about her upcoming marriage. She spoke about being "set in her ways." Now she would have to share her living space, reorganize her priorities, and generally uproot the stable life she had created for herself. She wasn't sure that she wanted to be as flexible as marriage demanded. In this situation, planning for marriage meant that Elaine and her fiancé had to give particular attention to blending two well-developed lives in a way that honored each person's individuality yet allowed them to join together as a team to build a life as wife and husband. Negotiating this new life-cycle phase simply required a bit more attention due to the added stress of being out of sync.

Stress also occurs when people try to handle life-cycle demands they are not ready to handle. This explains why we often hear statements such as, "I just wasn't mature enough to handle being married back then," or, "Parenting just overwhelmed me when I was younger, but I'm much better prepared now."

So it is important to handle life-cycle tasks in an appropriate and timely manner, but it is also important to be aware of your own limits and to avoid making commitments like marriage and parenting until you are strong enough and mature enough to handle them.

Principle 4

Family life will be less stressful when cultural variation and change are attended to and affirmed.

Culture is a tremendous force in shaping a family's life together. Within each culture, and within each period of history within each culture, developmental timetables and tasks will vary. In many cultures throughout history, becoming a parent in one's later teens was the normal and accepted pattern. But today, teen pregnancy in America is not only out of sync with our cultural norms, it is fraught with stress and risk. More than likely, a teenage mother will be unprepared physically, emotionally, socially, and economically to parent a child. She, her family, and especially her child will more than likely face a turbulent and uncertain future.

As another example, consider the age at which children are expected to move out and start living on their own. Some Irish-American families may encourage young adults to be living on their own by their midtwenties regardless of marital status. Yet in some Asian-American families, members may be expected to remain in the nuclear household until marriage. In other homes, particularly those of Italian-American and African-American heritage, there may be no expectation either way. These variations are not a sign of developmental abnormality. Rather, they remind us that the timing of many family developmental stages may vary according to individual needs as well as family and/or cultural preferences.

Difficulties may occur within a family when we or our children begin to adopt the values and expectations of the dominant culture, even though those values and expectations are at odds with the family's cultural expectations. This most often occurs in first-generation immigrant families, where the values and norms of the country of origin clash with American expectations. This is a natural part of the acculturation process as newly arrived families face the challenge of retaining their own cultural heritage while also incorporating the skills necessary to adapt to life in America.

Cultural clashes do not always occur between two different cultures. They may also occur within one's own culture, which is in a constant state of flux. Here in America, we are seeing a shift in the length of time adult children remain in the home. For financial reasons, it is not uncommon for children to return to the nest after college. As we've become a much more technologically advanced society, college often becomes merely a prerequisite to graduate school. Unable to support themselves, young adults postpone marriage and remain with their parents longer than was common a decade or two ago.

Such changes are not uncommon. In fact, each time period in history reflects subtle changes in how life is understood and defined.

Principle 5

Family life will be less stressful when the family has sufficient time to absorb the impact of one stage prior to movement into the next stage.

Have you ever played one of those video games in which you are constantly bombarded by objects flying at you from all directions? You finally get to the point where you think you're safe, only to be set upon by a host of new attackers.

Sometimes family life is like that. You barely have time to catch your breath before you're suddenly hit with a new challenge or crisis. The result can be devastating.

Rapid-fire challenges may occur for a number of reasons. A reconstituted or blended family, for example, may have many stages and transitions all going on at the same time. The parents are negotiating a new marriage, the children are finding their way in a new family, and each individual is also facing his or her own life-cycle challenges. If you are in a newly blended family that has teenagers in it, you know exactly what we're talking about. There is insufficient stability because things are changing so fast and the family doesn't have time to establish a secure sense of itself.

Another example of this occurs when adult children move back home. Consider what happens to the couple who assume they are finally on their own, having just said good-bye to their youngest child, when all of a sudden their thirty-four-year-old married son shows up at their doorstep with all of his belongings. It seems his wife has kicked him out because he drank too much and was irresponsible with family finances. Now what? These older parents certainly didn't expect to have their son back home again. And the suddenness of his arrival did not allow for an adequate period of transition between one stage and the next.

Sometimes a family tragedy may prevent people from offering adequate attention to family and individual developmental needs. When a family member is ill or dying, it is necessary and appropriate for the family members to direct their energies to care for that individual. But still, time marches on, and sometimes added stress is present as the developmental needs of other members of the family are neglected.

Gretchen discovered this as she was caring for her terminally ill husband, Dave, who was only thirty-five. A nonsmoker and a physically fit man, Dave nevertheless suddenly fell ill and his condition was diagnosed as advanced lung cancer. Gretchen immediately turned her attention to caring for her husband, finding him every available treatment possible. Meanwhile, the couple's twenty-month-old daughter, Aimee, found herself without Mom and Dad most of the time. And when they were home, Aimee saw her mother caring for her weak and dying father.

This young family was in the midst of a terrible tragedy. Gretchen needed to focus her energies on Dave, but she felt guilty that she was neglecting her daughter. One night in a prayer service, she broke down in tears over how much she was neglecting Aimee.

The group assured her that the little girl was being well cared for by Gretchen's mother, who lived with the family. A host of friends and family members also took turns providing meals for them, and many within the group spent some time every week caring for Dave and Aimee to relieve some of the pressure Gretchen was feeling to "be all things to all people." The group members tried to assure her that, while Aimee was not yet capable of fully grasping what was happening, she was watching her mother lovingly take care of her father, and that would provide her with a gift she could always carry with her, even after her daddy was gone.

While appreciating this encouragement, Gretchen was also moved by the distress she was seeing in her daughter. At that moment, she went to the nursery and brought Aimee into the prayer circle with her. The little girl clung desperately to her mother and cried out if anyone so much as tried to touch her mommy. She needed her all to herself. The group continued to pray as Aimee nestled in her mother's lap.

In the days ahead, as Dave's illness progressed and Gretchen became even more focused on caring for him, their community of support rallied around them. People continued to bring meals every day. They organized house-cleaning brigades and sponsored a video night for Aimee and her young friends. When Dave died, the support continued, lessening only as Gretchen was able to give full attention to mothering and household responsibilities.

This family illustrates how we must sometimes put certain needs and routines on hold, even though that may have a severe impact on other family members. Aimee was stressed out. She was going through a time when she could not get what she needed from her mother and father to ensure her safety. Gretchen knew that things couldn't be normal for Aimee during such a time of crisis, and that meant she would have to take the time later on to go back and tend to Aimee's fear and need for connection. This was the only way the little girl could deal with the new developmental challenges that greeted her each day.

It's not only in families who are dealing with crisis that there is insufficient time to deal with one developmental stage before moving on to the next. This also happens in growing families where children are passing through different stages of development at the same time.

A mother of three children comments that she was "up to her elbows in diapers and temper tantrums" for seven years! As each child graduated from diapers, a new child was born. Thus, while one child was going through the power struggles that come with toddlerhood, the younger child was in the diaper stage.

It's easy to sympathize with this mother. She must have felt like the lead character in the movie *Groundhog Day,* who kept living the same day over and over and over again. When this mother finally saw the light at the end of the diaper tunnel, she was caught off-guard by the bittersweet feelings that accompany each child's leaving home for his or her first day of school. She was not prepared for this stage of development in her or her children's lives.

As a parent, you are likely to be constantly immersed in developmental phases—facing new challenges every day with little or no breathing room between events. Some of these rapid-fire events are avoidable, and some are not. But regardless of that, when you get caught in the cross fire, your energy can wear thin, and it is easy to lose your perspective.

When this happens, think of Gretchen, who was able to pause for a few moments to notice the strain the rapid-fire action was placing on her daughter. She made efforts along the way to let Aimee know she was not forgotten, and she committed herself to going back and tending to those family needs that inevitably got lost in the shuffle.

Principle 6

Family life will be less stressful when the family has sufficient internal resources—emotional, intellectual, psychological, spiritual, social, and material—to draw upon.

In chapter 3, as we studied three families who lost their husbands and fathers, we saw how those families' internal and external resources contributed to their handling of the situation.

The way you perceive an event is an internal resource. So is your basic character style and intellectual ability. Your faith is also a vital internal resource that offers strength and guidance. As was mentioned in chapter 3, a family's internal resources also include the level of interpersonal connectedness between family members as well as the adaptation strategies employed during times of stress. Internal material resources refers to the basic life necessities available to a family during times of stress—adequate nutrition, housing, transportation, financial resources, etc. Other internal resources come naturally, as the result of inborn abilities and traits. But for the most part, internal resources are built up over time as you tend to the individual and developmental tasks that we've discussed previously.

For example, people who are emotionally healthy when they enter marriage will be better able to withstand the ebb and flow of those stressful early years. Their marriage will grow strong if the partners are equally committed to nurturing their relationship. Parenting is less stressful when basic living expenses can be accommodated. And letting go of grown children is not so overwhelming when you have continued to nurture your relationship with your spouse and friends and when you have spent time developing your own interests and hobbies. And so it goes.

As we've discussed previously, internal resources alone are not enough. You also need external resources to draw upon. In Gretchen's case, her biggest external resource was the circle of other Christians who supported her with their actions, their prayers, and their continual encouragement. Gretchen was a strong woman who was heroic in the way she cared for her dying husband. But despite her obvious internal resources, she was also in desperate need of those external resources to carry her through that most difficult time.

As internal resources can be developed over time, the same is true of external resources. For instance, involvement in a church provides a support group to stand with you in a time of crisis. In the same way, a careful handling of the family's money—saving and making prudent investments—can help provide the financial resources necessary to carry you through a crisis.

Unfortunately, there are many ways in which external resources can be quickly depleted. The loss of a job, the sudden death of a spouse, or a devastating illness or injury may impair your ability to provide for your family. Or financial resources may be present, but you may not have access to other resources, such as a caring community.

Still, it is vitally important to develop your external resources to whatever degree you can, remembering that family health is not created and maintained in isolation. Just as the individual is part of and interdependent with his or her family, so too our families are part of and interdependent with the rest of society.

Families become increasingly vulnerable when we, as a community, turn our heads and only look out for our own interests.

You Are Not Alone

Over the next few chapters, we will seek to bolster your coping resources by offering added insight into the different challenges our families face as we go through life.

It may help to know that you are not alone as you face particular times of stress. But more than that, our goal is to lessen the stress by enabling you, with God's help, to make better choices as you seek to empower and strengthen yourself and your family during difficult times.

6

Starting Out on the Road to "Happily Ever After"

So they were married—to be the more together—
And found they were never again so much together,
Divided by the morning tea,
By the evening paper,
By children and tradesmen's bills.
—Louis MacNeice, "Les Sylphides"

The stanza from MacNeice's poem quoted above presents a pretty gloomy look at what life is like for married couples. Must that happen? Do the couples who start out with stars in their eyes, expecting to float through life on a loving cloud of bliss, have to wind up disillusioned and separated by the stresses of daily existence?

In the classic movie *It's a Wonderful Life*, we watch as George and Mary embark on their new life together as husband and wife. Their eyes sparkle as they move into this new, wonderful season of life. But it's not too long before children and other life events have combined to throw the happy young couple a curve or two. And it's only with the ultimate intervention of an angel that the family is able to survive.

Well, the truth is that we live on a planet that has fallen far from what God intended it to be. The result is that life is often hard, and love, in and of itself, is not always enough to protect a young couple from being battered by life's storms. But then again, it is possible to be prepared for those storms and for the pain that often accompanies them.

Bear in mind that when we talk about storms, we are not necessarily referring to catastrophic events in the life of a family. There are plenty of storms in the ups and downs of everyday existence.

We've Only Just Begun

Talk with almost any engaged couple, and you will hear tremendous excitement and hope about what tomorrow may bring. Continuous waves of utter euphoria flow through their veins as their wedding date approaches. Despite the prewedding tension between themselves and/or their families, both the bride and groom imagine that their life together will come as close to paradise as is possible this side of heaven. They believe that their walk down the aisle will usher in their era of "happily ever after."

Then, a day or so after the honeymoon, they wake up to a new reality as they begin to encounter the many adjustments married life requires. Just for starters, there is the responsibility of setting up a new household and household routines. Who does the cooking? Who buys groceries? Who is responsible for household repairs? Whose family will be visited when the next holiday comes around? All sorts of decisions must be made that require a great deal of give-and-take—decisions with regard to budgeting and household expenses, careers and work commitments, how to spend leisure time, and so on.

Jana and Ben had a lot going for them when they were first married. They had gone together for two years, had the blessing of their parents and friends, both had good jobs, and, best of all, they were deeply in love.

They hadn't been married too long, though, before Ben's widowed mother, Mary, began making demands on them that seemed intrusive to Jana. Being the youngest and only son, Ben had been the one his mother had counted on for many years. After he was married, Mary felt lost and lonely.

Whereas Mary liked Jana, she couldn't understand why she was getting the cold shoulder whenever she called. Meanwhile, Ben was not able to refuse his mother's requests for help, which only increased Jana's resentment. Things finally blew up over plans to spend the Christmas holiday with Jana's family. Mary was distraught over the idea, and dramatically and emotionally made her feelings known. Unhappily, the result was that Jana went to see her family while Ben stayed behind to spend the weekend with his mother.

Among the many challenges faced by the newly married couple is the restructuring of family relationships and loyalties. Poor Ben needed to set limits with his mother. Instead, afraid of saying no to her, he allowed his wife to play second fiddle to Mom—an unfortunate and unwise decision.

Ben and Jana remind us of the normal, yet intense, struggles we all may face as we learn how to start a new family system. Each of us comes from families with their own ways of doing things, their own ways of viewing the world. Each of us comes with a bag of needs and expectations that we expect our wife or husband to fix and fulfill. Each of us has our strengths and weaknesses, our good and bad qualities.

Shortly after Bob and Joanne were married, the dishwasher in their apartment went on the fritz. Joanne couldn't believe her ears when Bob told her to call a repairman. Why, her father had never called a repairman in his life. Whenever anything went wrong, he just got out his toolbox and took care of it. Unfortunately, Bob had no aptitude for such things; in fact, the worst grade he ever got in school was in a shop class. You might say that Joanne was being unfair, but her expectations were only based on her experience.

Rita was shocked and upset to discover, shortly after their honeymoon, that Keith expected her to fix dinner every evening, even though they both worked. His mother had always been the "chief cook and bottle washer" when he was growing up, so it was only natural that he expected his wife to fill the same role. Rita, on the other hand, felt that they should share kitchen duties. She didn't think it was fair that she should be expected to do all the cooking, especially when she worked every bit as hard as her husband did.

These are just some of the types of problems that are likely to arise in the early days of a marriage, because both the husband and wife may enter the situation with unrealistic and unfair expectations of his or her partner.

The young couple has to learn to negotiate and cooperate on a number of fronts. They also need to learn to deal in love with the difficulties that may arise when

- he snores.
- she steals the covers.
- he leaves little hairs all over the sink.
- she leaves her pantyhose hanging in the bathroom.
- he spends too much time watching sports on TV.
- she wants to talk when he doesn't feel like talking.

These are just some of the difficult situations—and there are dozens more—that must be handled by the newlywed couple. And even though some of them may sound rather small, they can do great damage to a marriage, especially if tensions and resentments are allowed to build up over time.

The success or failure of working through these stressors will also affect the next stage of life: when a child is brought into the marital dyad.

And Baby Makes Three

The birth or adoption of a first child is a time of great joy but also a time of great tension for a couple. If a child comes into the family before the married couple has adequately met the challenges that arise from blending their two lives, the result can be disastrous for all involved.

A common source of difficulty surrounding the arrival of the first child is the time and attention involved in caring for a newborn. If the couple is not secure in their relationship, they may begin to resent the baby or their spouse for the amount of time and energy it takes to tend to the baby. The parents may try to disguise those feelings, but irritations will be there and they will eventually come out—especially when Mom and Dad are fatigued at the end of a long day, feeling financially pressured, or are troubled in some other way.

Many young couples underestimate the demands of a baby. Lynelle and Dion were looking forward to their first child. But then, their joy over the "blessed event" was tempered when the baby had colic. The infant's constant crying made them question their parenting abilities, which led to feelings of low self-esteem. When they couldn't comfort their little girl no matter how hard they tried, they became exasperated and angry. The level of their frustration unnerved the baby, who then cried even harder, which only added to the tension, frustration, and anger in the home.

Many factors can intensify or lessen the impact of these types of crises—as well as other challenges most families encounter. The first three factors involve the couple's relationship:

1. The maturity and experience of the couple.
2. The strength of the marital relationship.
3. Their co-parenting commitment.

These three items are perhaps the most important elements influencing a family's ability to navigate child-rearing difficulties. If Mom and Dad are incapable of standing back and looking at the needs of their child apart from their own needs, if they are engaged in battle after battle with each other, or if they fail to be mutually engaged in the care of their children, communication will break down, chaos will result, and everyone will suffer—especially the child.

The five remaining factors involve the family's support system and how well the couple uses those resources:

4. The support of extended family members and friends.
5. The resources available in the community.
6. The quality of the help offered.
7. The couple's ability to find and make use of this help.
8. The couple's experience with medical care and community support.

Some of the barriers couples face may be due to the limits of their family, friends, and community, while other barriers may be due to pride or a lack of assertiveness when it comes to seeking assistance. If a couple had positive experiences when seeking help in the past, they may be more energetic when it comes to seeking assistance now. But if, on the other hand, they felt shamed, disappointed, or ripped off, they will be hesitant to try again.

For Dion and Lynelle, one way to cope with their colicky baby was, first of all, to acknowledge the loss they felt about not having a calm, quiet, sweet baby. That dream and all the expectations that went along with it had to be properly grieved. It was also important for them to understand that their baby, too, had suffered loss. She had not enjoyed a smooth beginning to her life. She had physical pain that she could not understand and that could not be explained to her. Dealing honestly with the disappointment they felt helped Dion and Lynelle circumvent the negative blaming interactions so they could pull together to provide the secure, comforting environment their baby needed.

Also, as Dion and Lynelle came to see themselves as equal partners in the care of their newborn, they were able to arrange rotating shifts for her care. In this way, each parent was able to enjoy an occasional break for some peace and quiet. This type of partnership—with each parent sharing in the child's daily routine—also allowed each partner to express care and concern for the other. They did not become so consumed by caring for their child that they neglected each other.

When a couple is adjusting to the demands of a newborn, their extended family members and friends can be either a support or a hindrance. A newborn usually engages people and becomes the focus of attention at social gatherings and thus becomes an entry point into the welcoming hearts of the community. However, if a couple is shunned because they are unable to quiet their crying baby, they may feel rejected and even more isolated. The glaring, judgmental glances are a painful reminder to the couple that they are being kept outside the social circle. But when the crying baby is embraced, when family and friends empathize with the baby's pain and the parents' exasperation, all the members of the young family are nourished in the midst of their struggle.

Dion and Lynelle were also able to speak with their pediatrician about their search for possible causes or remedies for their daughter's distress. They also sought out the advice and support of friends and church members who had experienced similar situations. Sometimes just talking with other "veteran parents" can reassure a young couple that their feelings are normal, that they are not bad parents, and that it is possible to come through this difficult time with their marriage—and their sanity—intact.

They could, and so can you. You will be better able to handle the challenges that come your way as your children—and your family—pass through the other stages of life.

7

Small Children, Small Problems—Says Who?

"There's never enough time to do what we need to do!" If you know someone who says that, you probably know someone who has small children. Life is one busy whirl for parents who are dealing with the never-ending tasks that growing children bring into a family.

One woman put it this way: "I used to enjoy those relaxed mornings when my husband and I got up to have a leisurely cup of coffee with the morning paper. Now I don't get the coffee or the paper—period. I'm constantly attending to everybody's needs! When do I get a minute to sit down? I can't rest, because there's always one more thing to do."

If you are nodding in recognition, then you must have a little one or two around your house. If you don't yet have children, or if your children have not yet reached this stage—please read on. There is much to be said for the old Boy Scout motto "Be Prepared."

It might prepare you to know that when it comes to raising children, the pace can be stressful even when the activities are good. Such events as trips to the park, eating meals, bedtime rituals, visits to school, soccer practice, dance lessons, gymnastics, and so on can be exhausting.

Single parents may feel even more stress because they are solely responsible for taking care of all these activities, plus working full time and making day-care arrangements.

A single mother named Jacque gives us a brief look at a typical day in her life. "I get us off to school and work at 6:30 A.M. every day. The lunches have been made the night before, and I feel lucky on those days when I've gotten a good night's sleep because no one was sick during the night. The kids are bused to the day-care center, where I pick them up at 5:30 P.M. after I've been teaching all day. By the time I get there, I'm not sure if I have any emotional strength left to invest in my own kids after being with my students all day—and that guilt seems to take me down another notch."

Jacque goes on to say that her kids seem to act up at home as they release the energy that's been pent-up all day at day care. So it's quite chaotic while she's working on dinner. "It's frozen pizza again, because we have to get Curtis off to a baseball game, and Jake has a music lesson. So I'm working out a schedule of splitting my time between game, carpooling, and cleaning up the dishes. By the time I climb into bed, I'm thinking, 'Well, at least we made it through another day.' The one thing I feel sad about as my head hits the pillow is that I've had no time for adult relationships this week. I know this is taking a toll on me, but I can't see any way to make this happen while I'm so busy with my grade-school children."

Whew! Whether it's one parent or two, when there are young children in the home, life is never dull. The biggest question is how to have enough energy to keep going, and the biggest fear is wondering what will happen if you should run out of steam.

A common complaint registered by many parents during this phase of family life is a feeling of being empty, of having no time for friends, spouse, or leisure time activities. One mother told us she felt like a "mush brain" by eight every evening as she struggled to switch gears to interact in the adult world after her children were tucked into bed.

For parents like Jacque, whose work keeps them away from their children most of the day, there is often the added feeling of alienation and separation. Being away from their children for so much of the day leaves parents with a sense of disconnectedness, of not really being a part of the ongoing day-to-day life of the family.

Also, in families where one parent is able to stay home with the children, it's usually true that when the working parent comes home from a long, hard day, his or her energy is just as taxed as the other partner. Both Mom and Dad could use a break, and both are often disappointed when their spouse can't offer the relief they need.

All parents of young children are susceptible to being taxed beyond their limits. Successful coping often starts with simply acknowledging the struggle—admitting that it is often difficult, frustrating, sad, lonely, or confusing. That's not an admission that you're a bad parent. It is, instead, an admission that you *are* a parent.

It's okay to admit to yourself that you don't like the way things are right now and you wish they could be different. It's perfectly fine—in fact, it's healthy—to admit to yourself that you sometimes doubt the wisdom of the choices you've made or that you regret what sometimes seems to be a lack of ability to follow through on parenting responsibilities. Alcoholics Anonymous calls this "taking an honest inventory." It's not something that's done in the spirit of complaining but rather as a means of finding solutions to the problems that are confronting you.

Dwayne and Kathy, parents of two young children, discovered the importance of taking an honest inventory after they decided to seek counseling because of their "constant petty arguing." Dwayne took offense at Kathy's seemingly "superior" attitude regarding her parenting knowledge, while Kathy was constantly annoyed that Dwayne "displayed no common sense" when it came to "helping out" with the kids.

In counseling, as the two of them began to take a deeper look at the situation, they gained a new understanding of what was really going on between them. While this couple had decided that Dwayne would be the primary wage earner and Kathy would stay home to take care of the home and children, neither one of them was quite satisfied with the result of that arrangement.

For his part, Dwayne was beginning to see how much of his children's lives he was missing. In fact, when he came home from work he sometimes felt that he was "intruding" in Kathy's domain. As a result, he began to feel depressed and angry.

As for Kathy, she discovered she was resentful because she felt that her husband had abdicated his role as a parent and was leaving it all up to her. She also admitted that she did not trust Dwayne to do the things that she spent all day "planning and perfecting," such as cooking dinner and arranging time schedules for homework, chores, baths, and other activities.

Dwayne truly felt like an outsider, "incompetent and not needed," although he had never been able to express his feelings and desires clearly to his wife. Kathy felt overworked and unappreciated yet found it difficult to relinquish control. Likewise, she had never been able to clearly identify her ambivalent feelings—wanting her husband to be more involved yet being afraid to let him handle the parenting chores in his own way.

By clarifying their thoughts, feelings, and desires, Dwayne and Kathy were both able to see their predicament more clearly. Rather than viewing Kathy as a "know-it-all who simply did not trust him as a father," Dwayne began to appreciate the time and energy she put into caring for their children each day. He also began to see the role his own feelings of incompetence were playing in aggravating Kathy's suspicion of him. To combat this, Dwayne took responsibility for his fears and began reading some parenting books—books his wife had been urging him to read for at least a couple of years.

Kathy took a closer look at her reason for being so controlling and soon came to see that parenting was her identity. It was the only thing in her life that made her feel worthwhile. If Dwayne could do it as well as she could, she thought, then maybe nobody really needed her. So to maintain her own feelings of importance, she had set herself as the only one who truly knew how to care for the children. As she was able to work through these issues—which took time and courage—she began to let Dwayne be a true parent, with his own quirks, style, and strengths.

This couple also began to reexamine how each of their roles could be more flexible, not only to accommodate each other's needs, but the children's needs too. They both realized that the children needed to have their father take a more active role with them. They also needed to have a mother who was not completely stressed out all the time the way Kathy was when she was trying to do it all by herself.

Dwayne still went to work each day. Kathy still stayed home with the children. But as soon as he got home from work at night, they started viewing themselves as coparents. Evening tasks were divided and rotated to give each parent time with the children, and time for rest as well. Dwayne also decided that he would have more contact with the children by occasionally calling them from his office during the day. And he arranged to have them visit him at work every so often.

Kathy decided to enlarge the borders of her kingdom by exploring interests and hobbies outside of the home, by enrolling in an adult education class one night a week, and by volunteering her services at a local retirement community.

As a result of their effort to listen to each other's needs, Dwayne and Kathy have forged a deeper partnership. Today, it is apparent how much each values the other, not only as spouse and parent but also as an individual with unique skills, talents, and contributions to make.

As we said when we began this chapter, raising children is stressful, regardless of the way the family is structured. Often, as was true at first with Kathy and Dwayne, the typical human response to stress adds further strain to family relationships that are already taxed. But once you take the time to clearly identify the problem, perceptions can be clarified and broadened, and resources can be enlisted to provide solutions.

Perhaps the most important part of this process is intimate communication that strengthens your connections with your spouse and your children. It is always important to remember that to lead your children to growth and maturity, you must remain actively engaged in your own process of growth as well. Always.

Look Out! Here Come Teenagers!

A woman named Diane tells us that when her son, Steven, was three or four years old, he'd run into the house every time he saw some older kids coming down the street.

When she asked him what was wrong, he'd say, "There are teenagers out there. I don't like teenagers."

"But, Steven," she'd say, "you're going to be a teenager yourself someday."

He'd jut out his chin and say defiantly, "Not me. I'm never going to be one of *them*."

But you know what? He was wrong. He did indeed become a teenager, and as his mother said, "It seemed to happen awfully fast."

Well, the same thing is going to happen to your children. Or perhaps it already has. They will be sweet, cherubic angels one day, then the hormones will hit and full-blown adolescence will be raging out of control in your household. But take heart. Adolescence doesn't have to be the horror that some people have made it out to be. In fact, some people get ready for what they think will be a frightening and difficult time, only to find that these are the most wonderful years in the life of their family.

Some people fly through their children's teenage years, convinced that their parenting skills have ensured their success—while other parents spend a great deal of those years wondering where they went wrong.

The truth is that in some ways, teenage children are not so different from toddlers. Consider the average two-year-old, for instance. One moment, she is determined to do everything by herself. She doesn't need you and doesn't want your help or your advice. She's going to dress herself, even if she winds up with her pants on backwards, her shoes on the wrong feet, and a costume that's the most outrageous combination of checks, stripes, and dots you've ever seen! But a few minutes later, she is holding out her arms to you, wanting you to take her onto your lap and hold her—a baby again.

Teenagers can have the same mixed feelings. One moment, they're intent on being grown up, making their own decisions, and acting as if they know so much more than you do. The next moment, they act like scared kids again, running for the shelter of their parents' arms and wishing they could hold on to childhood just a little bit longer.

The difference for your children is that during adolescence the challenge of finding out who they are in relationship to the wild world out there is accompanied by an enormous (and rapid) physical, emotional, social, and cognitive growth spurt. One day they're children, and the next they're adults. The hormone surge that causes the voice to change, menstruation to begin, and acne to surface is a clear sign of the teenager's growing sexual maturity. But then again, by the time that happens, chances are good that you've been tipped off to what was going on by an increased interest in styles and looks and that cute guy or cute girl who seems to occupy so much more of their time and attention than their schoolwork!

When your authority begins to be challenged on a more frequent basis, and your children begin demanding increasing freedom, you can be certain that the adolescent years have arrived. One mother told us that when she drove her thirteen-year-old daughter to school, the girl wanted to be dropped off two blocks from school—obviously so none of her friends would see her riding with her mother in the old family car. Mom was hurt by it, naturally, but it helped her to understand that this is common behavior for teenagers of both genders. In fact, we'd go so far as to say that most teenagers act embarrassed by their parents at one time or another. It doesn't mean they don't still love you and need you. They do, but they want their friends to think they're more grown-up and self-sufficient than they really are.

A father reports that his teenage son is forever telling the family how to do things. He knows so much better than anyone else in the family how to handle every situation that comes along, and his advice comes dripping with condescension and sarcasm. Unfortunately, this too can be a common trait of the teenager of the species.

When this type of thing happens, you would be well-advised to remember the words of Mark Twain, who said that when he was a young man, he thought his father was ignorant and uninformed, but that when he was older, he was surprised by how much the "old man" had learned in the interim. So you see, this too will pass.

In the meantime, no wonder parents of teenagers worry for their children's safety. Their moodiness and idealistic view of the world, coupled with the blinding energy of their budding sexuality, makes for a vulnerable combination. No wonder most parents doubt the wisdom of their teens' choices and breathe a sigh of relief every night when they're tucked safely into bed.

The very things that cause us such concern are the challenges we long for our children to master. We want them to have a healthy sense of self and of their own identity, a healthy respect for their sexuality, and an ability to form caring, intimate relationships. We want to see them develop and flex their critical thinking skills, to give us a sign that they are intelligent and capable. We hope that these skills will guide them into meaningful work or a career so they can sustain themselves as adults. Everything we do as parents is to guide them to—and through—this transition from childhood to adulthood. But on the eve of their adult birth, we stand shaking and trembling.

The fact is that nobody has ever learned to walk without falling down a few times. Nobody can learn to run gracefully without suffering through some awkward strides. And nobody becomes an adult without experiencing times of uncertainty, disappointment, and perhaps pain. You cannot, and really should not, try to protect your children from every trauma of the teenage years, because it is often the traumas that help them grow and develop.

Still, all parents want to minimize the frequency and severity of those traumas. But how? Being too strict and controlling is not the answer, because the teenager must learn how to assume more and more responsibility for his or her own choices. Permissiveness is not the answer, because that is abandoning children when they most need your protection. What is a parent to do?

Perhaps you fear repeating the mistakes your own parents made—especially when you are hit by the shocking realization that you are sounding and acting more and more like them. You hear the things you say, the tone in your voice, and recognize them in your words, actions, and attitudes!

Remember, You're Facing Challenges of Your Own

It may help you, first of all, to remember that being the parent of a teenager is almost as difficult as being a teenager yourself. Whether you like it or not, the developmental phase of your child's adolescence is also a time when you will be challenged to grow and develop in various ways. Often, you'll have to look in the mirror and face your own developmental tasks, the ones you've always managed to skip over before. Your teenagers are challenging you to grow right alongside them!

Reflect for a moment on your own transition years. How did your parents respond to your emerging sexuality? Did they talk about and celebrate the changes that were happening to your body, along with the changes in your social status and interests? Or did they simply try to pretend that nothing was happening, showing discomfort with the changes in your body and your emotions through their silence. Did your parents push you into dating before you were ready, or did they treat every date with suspicion? As you grew, did your parents give you increasing freedom to correspond with increasing responsibilities? Or were you given too many responsibilities without the freedom—or vice versa?

It may be difficult for you to critique your own parents during this stage of life, especially when you realize how difficult parenting teenagers can be. Perhaps you admire them more than ever for standing firm during your own difficultness. Or perhaps it is clear now where they made serious mistakes with you. Remember that it was during your teen years that you developed attitudes about your identity and sexuality, that you found out whether it was okay to have your own values and opinions—whether you could differ from your parents and still be loved and accepted. When you made mistakes, as all adolescents will, were they treated as opportunities for growth and development, or were you shamed and humiliated by your foolishness?

As you look back on both the good and bad ways your parents acted during your teenage years, you are bound to see reasons for your actions as a parent—most likely including some things you'll want to change. Many times, it is not just our love and concern for our children that drives our decision making as parents but the residue of our own experiences that clouds our judgment.

When their children are teenagers, most parents often find themselves forced to come face-to-face with their past as the dynamics from their family of origin come crashing to the forefront. This, along with the added demands of parenting a teenager, can increase the stress in a marriage and also renew old, seemingly long-forgotten tensions with parents. And while your teenagers are pushing you in new ways, so are the challenges of being a middle-aged adult. Your own developmental cycle does not stand still just because the needs of your teenage children have demanded center stage.

Once again, we see the truth that when one family member is being challenged in some way, the rest of the family is also being challenged. The challenges your adolescent is facing are your challenges as well.

Competing Forces

When your children were young, you may have fretted over how best to discipline them. As they grew older, the question became harder and harder to answer. To paraphrase Shakespeare: "To be too strict or not strict enough? That is the question."

Sometimes the dilemma comes from parents who were overcontrolling or overpermissive. We don't know what an appropriate curfew is because we never had one or because the one we did have was extreme. When this was your experience, you run the risk of doing as your parents did out of a benign sense of loyalty—or even from misplaced retaliation. For example, you may have the attitude that "if I had to be in by 10 on Saturday night, then that's certainly good enough for my kids." Or you may react out of childlike resentment, becoming too permissive because "I'll never force my kids to come in early on weekends. I remember how much I hated that!" In both of these instances, decisions are being made for the wrong reasons instead of by giving proper consideration to what is best for all concerned.

Other times, parents revert to an overcontrolling or wishy-washy style of parenting because "the world is different than it was when I was a kid," so they simply don't have any clear answers. They prefer an early curfew on weekends because the world seems to be a more dangerous place than it used to be. Or given what their children have experienced or been exposed to, they may mistakenly view their kids as being much more adultlike than they were at that age, therefore giving them too much freedom—freedom they may not yet be ready to handle.

So how do you ease your way through these competing influences in your search to find what is appropriate for your teenage children? In our book *The Family: A Christian Perspective on the Contemporary Home*,[4] we explore in greater detail the family processes that can empower your children. We examine biblical themes of how God interacts with us and then apply those themes to our relationships with our spouses and children. We also examine what contemporary research has to say about the keys to successful parenting. While there is no one correct way to grow healthy children, we found that parenting styles which are high in structure and nurturing support are the most conducive to developing competent, secure adult children. By *structure,* we mean parenting that communicates clear rules and instruction that teaches appropriate behavior. By *nurturing support,* we mean parenting that clearly conveys love, warmth, and security. Does it sound like walking a tightrope? Yes, parenting often takes on the image of the circus high-wire act. And your teenage children are the ones who need you to provide the security of a safety net.

Let's take a closer look at what we mean by structure. It is not the same thing for a fifteen-year-old as for a ten-year-old. That younger child may be given a hard-and-fast rule that she is to be in bed every night by nine, lights out. But the fifteen-year-old should gradually be learning how to take responsibility for her own body's need for rest. When a parent communicates to a child, "We'd like you to be in bed by ten, since you have to get up at six," and then leaves that responsibility to the child because "we think you're old enough to make those decisions," the teenager is given greater freedom to be responsible. If she abuses that freedom and is too tired to pay close attention in school the next day, she is then paying the consequences for making irresponsible choices.

Bedtimes, of course, are a relatively risk-free zone. What about curfews, dating, parties, and so on? In these areas, each parent will make different choices based on what he or she thinks about the teenager's friends, sense of responsibility, and the situation presented. But at the same time, every parent must begin to let go. You have no choice but to accept the fact that your children will take some risks and make some decisions you don't agree with. But this is when they most need your constant loving support—to know that even if you disagree with the choices they've made, you will always love and accept them.

Traveling to the Beat of a Different Drum

Most parents' dreams for their children come bursting forth during the teen years:

- We want them to excel in academics, sports, and other activities.
- We want them to be popular.
- We want them to have a strong, vibrant faith.
- We want them to go on to college, where they will prepare to make their mark as doctors, attorneys, scientists, and so forth.

But what happens when your child wants no part of such things? What if the boy you've always wanted to be a sports star prefers ballet instead, or the girl you hoped would be a cheerleader wants to try out for varsity football? Maybe there's no desire to go to college—and finishing high school is even in doubt. Or what if you learn that your child is struggling with his or her sexuality? What if, in the confusion of adolescence, your child develops a substance-abuse problem, is promiscuous, or becomes pregnant?[5] What if your child disappoints you and lets you down in ways you never thought possible?

How can you find a way to love and support your child through such difficulties? And how can you navigate your own way through them?

The first thing you must do is come to terms with your own disappointments, grieve for the child you always imagined you would have. When you finally understand that your children are not extensions of you but people who are unique and distinct, then you can begin to discover who they are—even to admire their differences. Once that happens, it will be possible for you to stand with your children in love and support, offering them guidance in ways that empower who they are.

A woman named Mary told us that she was having a terrible time coping with the behavior of her older daughter, Lindsey. Lindsey was not at all like her younger sister, Lisa, who loved all the traditional "girl stuff." Whereas Lisa loved to wear dresses and play with her dolls, Lindsey could most often be found climbing trees and playing ball with the boys. Mary tried hard to accept her daughters' differences and to love them as individuals. But there were still problems, and they usually came to a head on Sunday morning when Mom wanted her daughter to wear a dress for church and Lindsey insisted on wearing jeans.

The same battle raged every Sunday morning, until Mary began to explore why she was so emotionally invested in making her daughter wear a dress. As she did that, she came to see that she wanted her daughter to be like her. She also believed that her daughter's appearance was a reflection of her skill as a mother. At thirteen, Lindsey was becoming a beautiful young lady, and Mary wanted to "show her off." For her part, Lindsey just wanted to be herself. She felt more confident and comfortable wearing pants and resented having to dress up in "a costume" to please her mother.

Once Mary began to let go of an expectation that was based on her own self-interests, she was able to affirm Lindsey's unique style while, at the same time, offering guidance. No, the jeans were still not okay for Sunday, but she would help Lindsey find dress pants that suited her tastes. In this way, Lindsey felt respected and affirmed by Mom's limits.

Another woman expressed how hurt she was when the youngest of her three boys decided against attending college. This woman's husband was a surgeon, she was an attorney, and the couple's two older boys were apparently set to follow in their parents' footsteps. One was in graduate school at a prestigious university, and the other was preparing to enter medical school.

But Tim had no interest whatsoever in academia. He was a wonderful carpenter. He had a natural ability for working with wood and made beautiful cabinets, dressers, and other furniture.

Although it was a somewhat difficult process, Mom finally had to come to see that her youngest boy was doing what he was best suited for, that he was following the path that would bring him the most success and happiness. She also came to see the worth and beauty that a person can gain from working with his hands. She had to understand that her son was by no means a failure but was, instead, gifted in his own, unique way.

Using Rituals to Empower

One way to prepare for and even celebrate adolescent growing pains is through the use of rituals that mark the passing of childhood and welcome the changes that lie ahead.

One couple, Jim and Sandy, parents of two daughters and a son, have told us about a series of rituals they have created to celebrate their family's passage through adolescence. The rituals, or special events, begin with an exclusive camping trip each child gets to take with their parents when they turn eleven. The children know years in advance that the event is going to happen and look forward with anticipation to "their own camping trip" with Mom and Dad. While the weekend is filled with activities of special interest to that particular child, time is also set aside for specific discussions regarding the significance of turning eleven and the years ahead.

Jim and Sandy say that while sex education has been a part of their family life since their children were babies, talk regarding sexuality takes on a new dimension with the adolescent. Sandy recalls sitting around the fire one night and sharing with her oldest daughter, Jaimie, about the pressures she felt as a teenager to have a boyfriend and to say yes when she wanted to say no. Already Jaimie could relate because of the pressure she was feeling from her peers. Together, mother and daughter explored possible choices Jaimie might face in the years ahead and talked about creative ways she could respond to pressures without giving in to them.[6]

Jim and Sandy say that while sexuality and peer pressure top the list of things to be discussed, time is also taken to reflect on childhood, examining both the good and the bad. This topic allows the parents an opportunity to safely explore some of the mistakes they've made, to make amends, and to model that even parents can make mistakes. This trip down memory lane also serves another purpose. When family members tell stories of their life together, the bonds of love are reaffirmed, providing strength and connectedness that will serve them well in the years ahead.

When the time came for their son's weekend, Jim and Sandy decided to play "This Is Your Life." Each participant, including their son, Rob, pulled together a script recalling fun and touching moments concerning the interactions they've had with one another.

Said Jim: "Rob reads me like a book. He opened his sketch by doing his best imitation of me when I'm mad—how I grumble and flail my arms when I've 'had it up to here.' He had us in stitches. Then he shared his memory of the day we found our family dog dead along the side of the road. Together, Rob and I buried Sam in our back yard.

"Rob recalled how, as we knelt beside the freshly dug dirt, I thanked Jesus for letting us have Sam and for giving him a happy life. Rob just melted into my arms and cried. That night by the fire, he shared how much that prayer meant to him. I shared how glad I was that we could be there to support each other in painful times. This time, we all cried—not just in remembrance of Sam, but because of our love and appreciation for each other."

While many other topics are discussed, Jim and Sandy also take time out to talk with each child about the tensions that may arise in the coming years as that child becomes more independent. They make a special point of affirming the child regarding his or her growing maturity and explain that tension may be a normal, yet temporary, part of this growing process. The weekend concludes with a sense that together they are all embarking on a journey full of exciting twists and turns, a journey which will culminate in that child's graduation into adulthood.

Over the next few years, Jim and Sandy continue to pay special attention to milestones in the lives of their children—going to a first dance or on a first date, getting a driver's license, and so on. They also celebrate increasing responsibilities. For instance, as the children turned thirteen, they were expected to start washing their own laundry. While this was a welcome relief for Jim, who had the responsibility of doing the family's laundry, it also signified the adolescent's continuing process of taking responsibility for his or her own needs. To mark this "rite of passage," each child was presented with his or her very own clothes hamper on the big birthday—one they got to pick out themselves, of course.

Throughout childhood, the three children had often been included in meal planning and preparation, but now, as teenagers, each child was to plan and prepare a meal one night a month. In this way, the parents got a night off while their teenagers practiced their culinary skills.

Activities such as these not only teach valuable daily living skills but also give teenagers the sense that they are important contributors to the home. In this way self-esteem is bolstered, to the benefit of all concerned.

There is no guarantee, however, that such activities will turn your children into angels. Some parents do everything right, only to see their teenagers make destructive choices. There are no guarantees. But at the same time, it is true that effective adults are, for the most part, those who were actively engaged in healthy relationships with their parents as they were growing up.

The relationship your kids have with you is their link to life. And the best insurance a family can have of surviving adolescence is to begin building strong and supportive relationships from the moment children are born. If that hasn't happened, it's important to commit yourself to repairing those aspects of the family relationship that have been neglected.

8

The Pain of the Empty Nest, and Beyond

Do you remember when you left home for good? Were you excited? Scared? Did your mother cry? And how about your father? Did he yuck it up and pretend that he was glad to see you go, while beneath his smile you could see his chin quivering ever so slightly?

No doubt about it, leaving home can be one of life's most memorable and traumatic experiences, both for the one doing the leaving and for the ones being left.

Ginny remembers crying continuously for four hours as her father drove her to the college she was going to attend. Finally, convinced that the tears were never going to stop, her dad pulled off to the side of the road and asked her if he should turn the car around and head for home. Ginny was about to fulfill her dream, but she had never anticipated the feeling of terrible homesickness that would engulf her on this big day in her life.

James remembers that he was shocked by his mother's emotional reaction when they said good-bye at the airport as he left for an extended stay in India. Not only was he saddened by his mother's grief, but he also felt guilty and a bit embarrassed that he didn't feel the same way. He tried, but he honestly had no idea how to respond to his mother's grief.

Janice remembers standing outside an empty apartment, watching her parents drive off in their car, which was loaded down with all of her belongings. She was moving across country to live closer to her boyfriend. And as she felt her heart racing within her, she wasn't sure if it was from fear about being on her own for the first time or from her great excitement about the adventure that awaited her in California.

You may remember similar tugs on your own dependence/independence strings the day you left the warmth and safety of your parents' home. It's an awesome task to move out into the world and begin building a life of your own.

On the Edge of Insecurity

Thomas Wolfe wrote, "You can't go home again," and to a certain extent he was wrong. Many young adults return to their parents' homes for refreshment and encouragement after they've made their way into the world. Some even come back home as adults when calamity of one type or another strikes them. But in a deeper sense, Thomas Wolfe had it exactly right. Once you leave home, it will never be the same. It will look different, feel different, and you will never have the exact same relationship with your parents.

Nothing is more disorienting than coming back into the home where you grew up, going into the room where you spent so much time, and thinking, "Something is wrong here. It doesn't look right." What has happened? Only that you have changed. Your perspectives are different now. Nothing looks the way it did to you when you were a child.

To a teenager, leaving home is a trip right to the edge of insecurity. It means Mom and Dad are no longer there to respond immediately to skinned knees, nightmares, or broken hearts. The newly "free" teenager or young adult may fluctuate between wanting the security of a parent's protection one moment and wanting to be totally self-sufficient the next.

Parents usually feel the same way. On the one hand, they're glad for some peace and privacy. On the other hand, they'd like a little noise and a little bit of a mess. They may be relieved that they are no longer responsible for their adult children, but they are also likely to be conflicted and saddened by the separation.

As we mentioned earlier, leaving home is not necessarily a sign of maturity, just as staying home is not a sign of immaturity. And so an important question arises: How do you know when a child is ready to be out on his or her own?

The answer is that teenagers and young adults are ready to leave home after they have achieved a certain level of what we call differentiation—both within themselves and externally in regard to their relationships with others. The following gives some examples of what it means to be differentiated. A differentiated person

- continues developing a clear self-definition as evidenced by life's goals and values.
- is able to establish a degree of intimacy in his or her own interpersonal relationships.
- separates his or her personal emotions from the emotions of others (in other words, knows how *he* feels about things instead of letting others tell him how he feels).
- trusts her own judgment but is able to listen to and weigh input and advice from others.
- accepts and appreciates the fact that others may have a different view of the world.

- can be informed by differences rather than threatened or controlled by them.
- is able to tolerate discomfort and conflict in relationships.
- takes responsibility for his or her own actions.
- cares for and nurtures himself or herself.
- is able to set limits that protect, nurture, and enhance.
- is able to care for and nurture others in ways that empower them.
- is able to identify and take responsibility for his or her own weaknesses and mistakes—accepting current limits while still believing in the ability to grow and change.
- can tolerate—not condone or condemn—the weaknesses and mistakes of others while still believing in their ability to grow and change.

Becoming differentiated is not something that happens overnight. It is not even something that can be expected to be accomplished in full by the time a person reaches young adulthood. Instead, it involves a process that begins the moment we are born and continues until we take our last breath. But at some point we must become differentiated enough so that we can separate from our parents and develop our own lives.

For the young adult, differentiation means that you are more confident of who you are—more able to set and pursue personal goals. It is reaching the point where you can admit that your parents are not perfect but, recognizing that, can refrain from blaming them for all your troubles. It's the ability to take responsibility for your own actions.

Differentiated adult children have established lives of their own, separate and apart from their parents. They usually have a separate residence, are financially independent, emotionally autonomous, and have their own personal support system. They have independent ideas, a clear sense of worth, personal purpose and meaning, and are committed to a lifestyle that is compatible with their personal values.

Differentiation is a process with many layers. Initially, most of us leave home in a symbolic, physical way. This is an important part of the process, the beginning stage of differentiation from our families. But the psychological differentiation from our families—which is the true essence of differentiation—often takes place much later in life. Some people who are in their thirties and forties have yet to reach that milestone.

When we talk of differentiating ourselves from others, it can sound as though we are defining emotional maturity and healthiness as a state in which you no longer need anyone else. That's far from the truth. The fact is that differentiation means having a defined sense of self that enables you to connect, relate, and interact with others. Only when you are truly your own person can you experience both self-sufficiency and true intimacy.

Differentiation does not trade intimacy for self-sufficiency but makes room for both. For example, it is when our children differentiate that we are able to become reacquainted with them as adult friends. This is when loving, mutually supportive friendships often develop. And by letting children go, parents gain a new place in their lives. No, your job as a parent will never come to an end, but its form will mature and change as your children move further along the process of differentiation.

When the Tie That Binds Becomes the Noose That Strangles

The process of personal differentiation can be a difficult, testy time for both parents and children; and it is a time when many unfortunate mistakes can be made.

For example, children who leave the nest prematurely often have unfinished business weighing them down. They thought they could solve all of their problems by leaving home, but instead the unresolved issues follow them into their new lives, where they continue to curtail self-discovery and growth until they are tended to.

Children who wait too long to break away may keep themselves dependent and unprepared to achieve a clear self definition. For them, unfinished business takes on a different form. Instead of running away, they hide in familiar surroundings.

When children are pushed out with little support or acknowledgment, as they hear the door lock behind them, they know that they face a cold and uncertain world. And when children leave overly dependent parents, they may feel guilty for "deserting" them. It is difficult to celebrate your new life when you are burdened with the thought that you are causing your parents pain.

Wendy, a young psychology student, told us how terrifying it was to realize that her mother, whom she considered to be her best friend, couldn't give her the freedom to be independent. Shortly after Wendy entered graduate school, some aspects of their relationship became so hurtful that her mother chose to cut off all communications with her daughter. They didn't speak at all for a month, and then they spoke sparingly after that. For two years now, there has been mostly a cold silence between them.

Wendy expressed her feelings about the situation in these words:

> I plead for freedom,
>   will fight for freedom.
> No longer is being with you the
>   fruition of my life;

My own freedom will be
  my fruition.
Manipulation and your withdrawal
  will not prevail.
I will blossom amidst your
  unceasing relentless darkness.
The storms you cast at me
  will not prevail.
You will never see ME,
  you will always see your me.
I am blossoming in your thunder,
  alone without you;
But eternally, eternally . . .
  I will choose freedom,
  my freedom.[7]

The period of separation became even more unbearable when Wendy became engaged and began planning her wedding. Her mother refused even to participate in the wedding, so Wendy missed out on the mother-daughter relatedness she had always dreamed would be a part of her wedding preparation. This was going to be the most important day of her life. A day to celebrate! Yet she was deeply saddened when she realized that her mother had slipped into the back row of the church as a passive presence rather than an active participant in the ceremony.

It would be terrific if we could tell you that Wendy's mother came to her senses and there was a joyous and tearful reunion. Such has not yet been the case, although Wendy still hopes that reconciliation will take place at some point down the road. She is making overtures in that direction.

But during these years of separation from her mother, Wendy has come to see herself as a woman in her own right, more than just someone's daughter. The distance between Wendy and her mother gave her an opportunity to develop a clear image of herself, to discover the woman God had created her to be—strong, assertive, and competent. Whatever happens in the future, Wendy must protect the self that has blossomed over the past few years. No matter how her mother responds at this point, she needs to maintain the integrity of her new sense of self.

When parents like Wendy's mother can't let go of their children, those children can have a difficult time achieving independence. It is hard to achieve differentiation in such circumstances, but it is not impossible. In fact, it is mandatory for the survival of the child.

Bringing Order out of Chaos

Differentiation is also hard to achieve for children who grow up in chaotic homes, in families where there is marital and/or parent-child discord—where the relationships between family members are dysfunctional in some way.

Vince is a young man who grew up in such a dysfunctional family, although he never realized it when he was a child. But as he grew older, he came to see that his family exerted a covert yet overwhelming control over his life—control designed to keep him "with them." Over time, Vince also came to see the unconscious roles he played that were keeping him from becoming his own person. As he looked at the ways he had always responded to his family, he began to see ways he could change his behavior and hopefully, the way the rest of the family members related to one another.

Vince wrote this account of how he worked to achieve differentiation in spite of the problems within his family.

"I thought I had grown up in a perfectly healthy home. I was a good son and the family peacemaker. Everyone counted on me to keep things smoothed out, and I obediently took on the role. It was how I ensured that I was loved and accepted. I was a great success, and everyone was pleased . . . until I began to establish a life of my own.

"The first protest came when I went away to college, the second when I married, and the third when my wife and I moved across country. It seemed quite normal at the time that there would be feelings of sadness, but as I look back I realize how much my independence threatened my family. Everyone was thrown off balance when I relinquished the role of being the caretaker. My family was more than sad; they were resentful.

"During our next visit, nine months later at the Easter season, my parents and I had a confrontation that would change the course of our lives forever. It was a traditional family celebration we all looked forward to. Alice (my wife) and I decided we would make a special effort to make sure things went smoothly. We thought we had made it through without an incident, until all hell broke loose the last night of our visit.

"While Alice, Dad, and I were finishing dessert at the dining room table, we heard Mother grumbling in the kitchen about not having enough time to be with me during the weeklong visit. I decided to talk to her directly, whereupon she took an offensive stance and began accusing Alice of taking me away from them.

"The strength of my mother's reaction made me question whether she was finally putting into words messages she had previously communicated via innuendo. She was jealous and angry that I had abandoned her to pursue a life of my own. She was no longer the center of my life, and she hated Alice for it. In my father's silence, I saw his passive support for my mother, a reaction that was all too common, yet just now understood.

"Alice was the one empowering person in my life! She had supported my attempts to become my own person and to follow my career goals in ways I had never experienced before. Yes, I had changed. I was becoming my own person. We left my parents' home the next day, defeated and demoralized.

"Over the days that followed, I paid close attention to my own reactions to this incident. I realized that I felt guilty for abandoning my parents. I felt like a failure and a traitor in their eyes. I feared that my whole family thought less of me for becoming my own person. Worse yet, I feared that by leaving, I would be responsible if anything happened to my parents. I was tempted to pull up stakes and move back home!

"There I was, enslaved by an unwritten family rule that stated, 'If you do what I want, you will be loved and accepted.' And I was all too ready to resume my caretaking role in order to not lose my place of 'esteem' within the family. I was ready to behave in a way that had helped me make sense of my world when I was a child but which had outlived its usefulness a long time ago.

"I instantly knew that moving back home was not an option. (Lucky for me, Alice wouldn't stand for it!) Realizing that I could not change my family, I began wondering if my only choice was to avoid them. But I was also assuming that I still had to play by my family's old rules: Do what they want, or don't bother coming around here. In my narrow way of thinking, I was assuming that my parents could not change, so why bother?

"I decided to try something different. I wanted a relationship with my family but not at the expense of my health and marriage. We all needed some cooling off after our Easter blowup; so for a time, our contact was minimal. As a temporary solution, this seemed appropriate, as I needed to sort some things out before I reapproached them. I needed to physically and emotionally disconnect for awhile so I could do some differentiation work 'in private.'

"It then came time to approach my parents. I was scared—no, I was terrified! What would I do if they wouldn't listen, if they wouldn't engage in a process of relating differently with me? I had to be really clear about why I was doing this, what I was hoping for versus expecting, and how I might respond if no progress could be made. I was setting myself up for misery if I demanded that they change. I was inappropriately placing responsibility for my emotional and relational health on my parents if I expected their response to solve all my problems.

"I was attempting to engage my parents in a process of healing and reconciliation because I love them. I was attempting to communicate with them about how I perceived our relationship because I believed in their ability to change. And maybe, just maybe, no one had ever given them the freedom and safety to be accountable for how they relate to others—to me in particular. Even though this process does require that hurtful events be talked about and acknowledged, my intent was not to punish or scold them for the hurtful things they had done as parents.

"When I felt clear in my mind about what I wanted to do and why, I called them and invited them to participate in some 'heart-to-heart' conversations with me. I acknowledged that all of us were hurting and told them I was wondering if they were willing to listen to my feelings as well as share with me their experience. An agreement to mutuality was the ground rule. They needed to be able to offer me their pledge to listen to me, while I needed to assure them that I wanted to hear their concerns as well. After wanting to know why I was initiating this—they feared that I was going to bash them for every wrong thing they had ever done as parents—to my surprise, they both said, 'Yes!'

"Over a period of a few years, my parents and I talked over the phone, in letters, and during our numerous visits. Many of our conversations were quite intense, but we were sharing honestly and intimately. I came to understand my parents' limits and to eventually accept them. I, in turn, must occasionally set limits with them as well, but now they understand what I am doing and why. As my parents grow older, I am experiencing them exerting more freedom—and courage—to love me for me. In many small ways they take interest in my adult life, affirming my accomplishments and supporting me in my struggles. I, too, provide them assurance of my deep love and appreciation for them. Once my parents were able to detangle some of our relational issues, they were able to see Alice for who she is—their daughter-in-law, whom they have come to appreciate."

Sometimes the Painful Choice Is the Right One

In a way, it's understandable why Vince's parents reacted to his moving across country the way they did. It's not easy to let our children go. It's hard to face the pain of separation. But some parents, in trying to avoid what hurts, make choices that create pain for themselves and their children that is more intense and more destructive than the normal pain of letting go.

Why does this happen? Every parent caught in this predicament will have a different answer to that question. But there is usually a common thread, which is that the loss of their children amounts to one more loss in life that these parents just can't face. The pain of this new loss threatens to blow the lid off all the stored up, neglected pain of previous losses. Keeping this common thread in mind, what are some of the other, overarching reasons parents find it so hard to let their children grow up and separate from them?

- Some find it hard to let go because their children gave them their only sense of identity.
- For others, the love and companionship of children was compensation for a marriage that was cold and unfulfilling.

- Some parents have trouble letting go of their children because their own lives have been fraught with struggle and pain, and they are jealous of their offsprings' freedom to pursue a happier life.
- Still others have never been alone and are afraid to make a life for themselves.
- Some have always had a distorted view of children, viewing them as possessions rather than as unique human beings.
- Another reason why some parents cling to their children is that caring for their little ones was a way to avoid confronting and caring for their own wounds.

All parents must face the painful reality that the (primary) child-rearing years eventually come to an end, that the children who filled their days with joy must leave to start lives of their own. It is a bittersweet experience to see children leave home. With their "becoming," we mourn a little bit of our own passing. But when we avoid our grief, shrinking away from facing our own life-cycle challenges, we become stuck in a form of emotional quicksand, and we drag our children down with us.

If you are a parent who is having trouble letting go, now is your opportunity to confront the losses in your life that may be hindering you and your children from going on. Grieving over your child's leaving may involve grieving over things in your life that have been painful and disappointing. It's important, in a situation like this, to seek out a friend, a pastor, or a counselor, someone you can talk with, who will help you see your way through something that is scary and uncomfortable. Surround yourself with supportive others who can remind you that it is in giving up that we receive, in letting go that we find. Bring your fears and your weaknesses before God, and you will find his comfort and strength. But you must actively want this and seek it out! God will work through people to help you, but it's up to you to open yourself up to the healing they can bring you.

If the choices you've made have driven a wedge between you and your adult children, you may have a bit of work ahead of you if you want to repair the damage— but most likely, it can be done. Most adult children are eager to forgive their parents of their trespasses, especially when they know those parents sincerely desire to make things right. The best way to start over is to talk with your children about your past mistakes and begin looking for ways to support and empower them today. Although it's risky, you cannot predict how your children will react, and this may be the only way to make a fresh start.

Now, not all leaving-home episodes have to be as traumatic as some of the stories we've recounted in this chapter. But just the same, all such experiences will be stressful because loss is involved. To make this loss less painful, both parents and children need to reach a point where they are able to let go emotionally while still keeping a connection that is mutually respectful and encouraging. It's important to come to the point where you can let the other person face his or her own personal pain without reacting to it in an extreme way or without thinking that it's up to you to fix it.

If you and your children (or parents) want to demonstrate empowering love, you must empathize *with* one another's pain, not protect each other *from* pain. When we spend our lives trying to protect others from feeling any sort of pain—whether those others are our parents or our children—we undermine them and ourselves as well. Often, it is through pain that growth occurs. To protect others from pain may be stifling their growth. Being differentiated means we'll be there to lend support but that we allow the other person to be fully in charge of his or her own life.

A man named Mike described his own leaving home this way: "It started by my pushing my parents away for a time. They stepped lightly for awhile, and gradually we let go of each other. It was a simple act of love."

Send Them Off with Your Blessing

It is also important for parents to let their children know that they leave home with the parents' blessings and love.

Martin, a single dad whose wife died when their daughter, Vickie, was just five years old, found it particularly difficult to see his daughter go. Not only was he sad to think of his "little girl" leaving him, but he was particularly troubled by the thought that his wife, Janice, had not been around to share the many significant events in Vickie's life. He ached when he thought about how much he wished Janice could see the beautiful person Vickie had become. The thought of his daughter leaving home brought back memories of all the times he sat alone at parents' meetings or during special award ceremonies acknowledging Vickie's success in life.

High school graduation day was hard enough for him to take, but the knowledge that his daughter was about to leave to attend college several hundred miles away was almost more than he could bear. The week before Vickie was to leave for college, Martin was overcome with feelings of sadness.

He couldn't stop thinking about the fact that this would be the last weekend they'd have together, the last pizza and video night, the last heart-to-heart talk, the last goodnight hug. All week long he walked around with a "big lump in his throat" that wouldn't go away.

A friend suggested that he needed to find a way to bring meaning to the event. After all, leaving home was not only an ending but the beginning of a new phase in their relationship. Whereas things would never be quite the same again, his friend challenged him to find a way to keep the bucket half full instead of empty. The idea was to develop a ritual that would celebrate Vickie's passage into a new time of her life.

Martin gave some thought to this and came up with an idea that saved the day for both him and his daughter. He decided to give Vickie a bookmark poem Janice had kept in her Bible before she died and which he had kept in his Bible since her death. The poem was special to him for two reasons. One, because it had meant a great deal to his deceased wife. And two, because it had Janice's handwriting on the back, along with some scribbles Vickie had added when she was a little girl sitting in a Sunday morning church service alongside her mother.

The last night Vickie was home, she and her dad spent the evening enjoying a favorite meal together. Then they finished packing and spent some time talking, laughing, and crying about other transitions that had taken place during their years together. After that, Martin gave his daughter the bookmark poem to take with her to college as a special symbol of the love he and Janice had for her. It was a transition object that marked the event with meaning for both of them. Vickie could take strength from her parents' union and hope from their Christian faith. She took the opportunity to express her own sadness about leaving but also affirmed her readiness to leave because of her father's faithful and wise guidance. The end result was a renewed sense of meaning about their past relationship and a better understanding of what the future would bring.

The next day, saying good-bye was not as difficult as Martin had thought it would be. As for Vickie, she left home knowing that she had her father's blessing—and her mother's too—in regard to her becoming a separate person, the very thing Martin had worked so hard to bring about.

You see, however our children leave home—whether it is with anger and disappointment over our inability to let them go, with fear and trembling over what awaits them in the outside world, with excitement over the challenges that lie ahead—whether they leave with ecstatic joy or with sadness and fear, it is a momentous day! It is their developmental destiny.

As we keep seeing, family pain is a normal part of growing up. The pain is sharper, more recognized, when it is encountered through an event—such as children leaving home—that forces us to make drastic changes in our behavior, our lifestyle, in the ways we relate to one another. These events produce strong internal reactions within us, often throwing us off balance for awhile. The launching of teenagers or young adults into the world is a powerful time when all family members are drawn to participate in an event.

Whether this is a relatively smooth transition or a rugged one, it requires letting go, grieving the loss, and in the process, tending to our own needs for growth and change. Only when we are able to do all of these things can we truly celebrate what the next phase of life brings for us, our children, and our family.

We look to God, the author and finisher of our life, to give us wisdom and strength as we deal with the good and the bad that comes with leaving; and as we look with hope, and with open arms, toward the future.

9

The Final
Letting Go

Mark's father was eighty years old, widowed, and lived alone. He'd always been in good health mentally and physically. He got up early every morning to take a walk around the neighborhood. He drove his own car, cooked his own meals, and even spent some time working in a little garden in the back of the house. He valued his independence, guarded it jealously, and had made clear on several occasions that no matter what happened, he never wanted to go to "an old folks' home."

Mark lived in another state, and it worried him that he wasn't closer so he could check up on his father more often. He tried to make up for it by getting his dad to come for extended visits, but his invitations were always met with a firm refusal. "I'm too old to travel," Mark's dad would say. "I'd rather stay right here at home, sleeping in my own bed."

Just recently Mark and his wife flew in to spend a week with Dad. Dad picked them up at the airport, and Mark relates: "I was sitting on the edge of the seat all the way home from the airport. It was frightening. It was obvious that Dad's reflexes aren't what they used to be. A couple of times he cut in front of other cars. When we got into the neighborhood where he lives, he drove for a while right down the middle of the street . . . and he seemed disoriented at times, even though Dad has lived in that neighborhood for more than fifty years."

That was only the beginning. When they got to Dad's house, they walked in to find the house full of foul-smelling smoke. Rushing into the kitchen, they found a pot with a few green beans in it sitting on a burner on the stove. The burner was going full blast, the beans were completely burnt, and the pot was ruined.

Dad just shrugged. "I do that sometimes," he said. "It's no big deal."

Later on, a neighbor told Mark that he had seen his dad out in the driveway one evening looking under the car, poking around in the bushes, obviously irritated over his inability to find whatever it was he was looking for. When the neighbor had gone over to see if he could help, Dad said he couldn't seem to find the newspaper "this morning." The neighbor gently told him that it was six in the evening, not six in the morning.

"It is? Oh, you know what, I must have fallen asleep in my recliner, and when I woke up I thought it was morning."

What is Mark going to do? He hasn't yet decided, but he knows he has to do something. It's obvious that Dad is slowly becoming incapable of taking care of himself. Mark understands his father's need for independence, but he also knows that if he doesn't take steps to change things, his father may wind up seriously hurting himself or, if he insists on continuing to drive, someone else.

It hurts to see someone who has always been a strong presence in your life begin to deteriorate. It's difficult to see physical strength fading—to see someone who has always been the epitome of reason and intelligence becoming arbitrary and confused. Yet age takes its toll on everyone, including parents.

Dealing with aging parents can bring about another of the most difficult and painful periods of a family's life together. Most of us want to believe our parents will stay "in charge" of their lives, but there comes a time when they are no longer coping as they did in the past. The magical thinking is over, and our childhood fantasies are dispelled because our parents have become frail and dispensable.

That's how it felt to Dave when his father, Howard, experienced a massive stroke right in the middle of preaching his Sunday morning sermon. A well-known preacher in his early fifties, his life was radically altered in a matter of moments. The left side of Howard's body was distorted, his face was contorted, and he was left without the ability to walk or talk.

It gripped Dave's heart, day after day, to witness his father's losses. Howard looked so pitiful when trying to express himself, and Dave felt his dad's agony when the man shouted out sounds in frustration over his inability to make himself understood. This man, who had been gifted with such profound speaking ability, who could move and stir others with his eloquent sermons, was now attempting to communicate through grunts and incoherent shouts.

As they sat together, a deep sadness reverberated between them. It was almost more than Dave could bear. This man had always been there for him, a rock of strength through every time of trouble, and now he was lying there helpless, unable to get others to understand or respond to his simplest request.

Undoubtedly, caring for aging or disabled parents can be one of life's most difficult experiences. The loss of a parent can leave you feeling anchorless and rudderless—as if a source of strength, protection, love, and guidance has been taken from you. Losing a parent can leave you feeling utterly and completely alone—especially if it happens suddenly, without time to properly prepare for the separation.

I Remember Mama

When your parent is taken without warning, you miss out on the chance to gently say good-bye, to wrap up loose ends, to squeeze in one final kiss and "I love you." Instead, you are left to work together those missing pieces through your memories of times together.

Kathy's mother died before Kathy was ready to have her go. The intimacy that had existed between them had been a rare and priceless experience. When Kathy lost her husband after just ten years of marriage, her mother was her source of strength and stability.

Kathy remembers: "When I was just a young girl, I remember how my mother and I lay together in a grassy meadow, watching the clouds float by overhead, laughing as we made out shapes and watched them change into other shapes. I felt so close to my mom and secure in her love. Sometimes we laughed and played together like two young girls. She would watch me roll down the hill, let out a howl, and come tumbling after me.

"When I was in my teens, I remember one warm summer night when we were sitting in the kitchen enjoying a chocolate cake. I talked on and on about my friends, dates, teachers, and the like. She was interested in hearing about my world, and I listened with interest as she talked about some of the experiences she had had when she was my age. Then, out of nowhere, it started raining. In a spontaneous, delightful moment, we decided to take a shower in the rain! We grabbed a bar of soap, ran out into our secluded back yard, soaped ourselves down and let the rain rinse us off. It was a wonderful moment."

Kathy continued to be close to her mother in the years following her marriage to her high school sweetheart, Larry. Her mom was there when Kathy gave birth to her son, Chad. And one year after that, she was there to hold her daughter's hand when Larry was diagnosed with lung cancer.

Kathy remembers, "The yearlong treatment was agonizing, but we had determined to fight and beat this disease. I couldn't imagine the cancer beating us but gradually came to see that we were losing the battle.

"That summer we spent three months at our family cabin on the lake with my mother. Larry was extremely ill. One day Mom sat next to me on the dock and we dangled our feet in the water, just as we had done every summer of my childhood. With the sun shining down on us, we lay back and stared up at the clouds floating past. It reminded me of that other, happier afternoon years before. But there was no laughter this time—only a sad, despairing silence.

"Then, so tenderly, my mother reached over, took my hand, and said, 'Kathy, Larry doesn't belong to you. You have to let him go.' The tears streamed down my face as she tightly held my hand. I needed her strength to help me open up my heart to let him go on with dying, to enable me to walk with him through this painful end of his life, of our life together.

"Little did I know that day that I would have to let go of her just two years later, when she died unexpectedly of heart failure.

"I often think of her when I look at the billowy clouds in the sky, for she was always a ray of sunshine in my life. She used to tell me that she sometimes pretended she was floating on a pink cloud with her feet dangling over the side, looking down on the world. Even now, I can picture her smiling down on me. And when the rain clouds come into my life, struggling as the single mom of a teenager, I know she is holding my hand. After that, when the rainbow comes, it reminds me of her colorful approach to life."

Life and Death

The stress of losing our parents is immense, but in many ways the stress of caring for elderly parents can be even worse. Sometimes drastic changes in the parent-child relationship coincide with other losses in life, such as adult children leaving home and lost hopes and dreams that may precipitate a midlife crisis. These losses, along with other events in our lives—such as our own health concerns, career changes, and financial difficulties—determine the difficulty or ease with which we are able to take on the task of caring for aging parents.

Regardless of what else is going on in your life, it can be terribly difficult to care for aging parents. There may be no one to relieve you when you're weary. It may be expensive. It may be time consuming, causing you to feel guilty because it seems that you are neglecting your spouse and children.

If your parents' needs are too great for you, you may be faced with guilt over having to bring in outside help—or over having to put your parents in a facility where they can get around-the-clock nursing care. Yet it is often necessary to reach for outside resources to help you cope with this particular challenge of family life.

Ironically, taking care of our parents at the end of their lives reminds us of the sacrifices they made for us at the beginning of our lives. It can be soothing to remind yourself of this when things get particularly rough—especially when aging parents may act like children. They may have grown cynical and grouchy over the years, they may be stubborn and less than gracious as you try to help them, and they may sometimes be unreasonable and unable to think with clarity. You're likely to be giving a lot without getting much in return. But there is no other way. These are the people who gave you life.

How can you care for an aging parent without becoming discouraged, defeated, and guilt-ridden? The only way is to take advantage of the resources that exist in your community to help you and also to enlist the aid of family and friends. Otherwise, you are likely to burn out and become resentful. Taking care of yourself while you are taking care of your parent or parents is the best way to counteract discouragement and defeat.

The following excerpts from the diary of a woman named Gerry clearly show some of the issues involved in caring for aging parents.

November 1982

She has arrived! She sits here in my living room chatting, and I am feeling less chattable. She is invading my space. It feels awful, and I wonder how I shall ever survive it. I feel ashamed of my thoughts! I must find someone I can share this with, or I'll resent her, I know.

January 1983

She is pretty good about making her instant coffee, toast with butter and jam breakfast. Today, I watched her go through the ordeal: Two pieces of bread in the toaster—push the lever down—go to the stove to heat water for coffee, back to the toast, push up the lever (toast isn't done), push it back again; look for cup, look for coffee, back to toast again. Now it is burnt. Take out the toast and put it aside, put in new bread, push down lever, back to coffee process, back to toaster, repeat the process, and get more burnt toast . . . take it out and try again. This goes on until she ends up with six pieces of burnt toast with the coffee. In the silence of my room I weep. I have such agonizing feelings about being responsible. I do not know if I can bear this alone.

February 1984

Bathing and changing clothes are increasingly a problem. She used to take her own clothes off and wash at the bathroom sink, but now she won't take her clothes off period. She goes to bed with everything on. It is now a battle of our wills. I set out new clothes each morning, and she ignores them. She refuses to bathe. . . . It gets more difficult day by day. She is winning the battle, and I am very defeated today.

October 1984

I decided to take her to a church choir concert tonight. She insisted on wearing her moccasins and took a many-colored blouse and put it on her head in the manner of a kerchief. She told me it was raining outside, and she needed it. I could not convince her that it wasn't raining. Walking up the church steps, I realized how absurd she looked. I wasn't sure whether to laugh or cry, so I did a little of both. I'm glad the church community was gracious to us. They have supported me in my decision to care for her, and it lifted my spirits when many greeted her with a kind and loving word.

July 1985

It's the Fourth of July. It is such a hassle to take her places, but I made another try. She argued about what chair to sit in, she was afraid the fireworks would fall on us, she didn't want to sit next to that old man, she hated the noise of the crying babies. She hates being dependent on me. It is perverse. I'm being my mother's mother and she's the little child, but she knows she is really not a child, and she rebels against this with all her might. No wonder we're both so confused and having such a difficult time of it. The counselor at the Elder Care Center helped me with this. She encouraged me to make sure I have my own peers as a support so I don't get stuck in my mother role.

September 1986

Today my mother had no words for me—just sharp silence. The source of the argument was my dog, Nikki. She loves feeding him the food she doesn't want to eat. She doesn't like it when I disapprove of her actions, so she is scolding me with her silence.

January 1987

She was so angry today, she made ugly statements. "Gerry, you're crazy! Gerry, you're dumb! Don't you know how to do that?" She seemed to need to put me down by being the critical parent. I am ready to scream back at her. She knows how to trigger all my buttons. There is no appreciation for what I am giving her. I can hardly contain myself. . . .

August 1987

She was in a rare mood today. She asked if I would like to wear one of her party dresses, since she saw that I was getting ready to go out for the evening. She loved to dance when she was younger but is too uncoordinated to do it now. Yet she swayed around the house in a dancelike movement with the radio music. She talked about how her father loved to listen to her play the piano. It was a bright spot in the very bleak, yearlong struggle of negativity.

January 1988

I went to check on her this morning and found her sitting in her chair with her clothes on. She was dead. . . .

She must have died peacefully; there was no evidence of struggle. I breathed a word of thanks for that. I placed a blanket around her and silently grieved her death. There were no tears but a deep, inner grief for the sadness of her life. I was glad to have this moment alone with her. I could admit that I felt free and at peace. I did my best to care for her in a loving way. I have learned much about myself in the process and have appreciated the people who have come into my life to care for me during this time.

Gerry cared for her mother even though the rewards were slim. Her mother was unable to receive the tender care Gerry had to offer because resentments from her past left her a lonely, isolated woman. From Gerry's diary, we can see how she got through the rough places with the help of friends and community resources. She knew that taking care of her mother was not time wasted, even though it was often a difficult task. Gerry's reward came from knowing that she did what she could to make the last years of her mother's life as pleasant as possible.

Parents in Crisis

Over the last few months, the difficulty involved in caring for aging and ill parents has hit home for the Balswicks—especially for Judy, who has spent three months at her parents' home helping them go through a family crisis. Both parents were hospitalized within two days of each other with life-threatening illnesses—her eighty-six-year-old father with phlebitis and her ninety-year-old mother with pneumonia and congestive heart failure.

The seriousness of Judy's mother's condition put an incredible emotional stress on her father, in addition to his physical condition. The impact of their dual illnesses also affected Judy's brother and sister and their respective families. But during this difficult period, aunts, uncles, cousins, friends, neighbors, and home-care nurses all did their part to help ease the pain. Below, Judy shares some personal reflections of this stressful time in all our lives.

A Change of Plans

We had been planning a great birthday celebration in Phoenix. It was going to be the highlight of our year to gather around our ninety-year-old mother to express our love and appreciation for her beautiful and fruitful long life. In fact, by every indication, it looked like it would be a good year for my parents. Mom's Parkinson's disease was in check, and both she and my father had been alert and energetic when I had seen them just months earlier.

That's why I was shocked when Aunt Cena called to tell me that both Mom and Dad had been admitted to the hospital. My brother and his family had already arrived in Arizona to celebrate Mom's birthday, and I said I would get there as soon as I could leave Toronto, where I was conducting a seminar on family relationships.

Unfortunately, the freezing Toronto weather was causing havoc at the airport. Planes were being de-iced while I listened anxiously to announcements about all the flights that were being canceled. I prayed I wouldn't be stranded and breathed a sigh of relief when the plane finally took off. I arrived in Los Angeles at 10 P.M.—1 A.M. Toronto time, which was my body's time. I was exhausted when I made it home an hour later.

Immediately, I checked my answering machine and heard an urgent message from Aunt Cena: "I think you ought to get here as soon as you can. Your mother is worse, and I don't know how much time she has left." I could hear the urgency in her voice, and given a new burst of energy by the adrenaline that flooded through me, I began repacking my suitcase, scheduled a flight for Phoenix, and headed back in the direction of LAX.

I prayed silently all the way to the airport that God would not take my mother before I got to Phoenix, that he would allow me to have some quality time with her. I was also worried about my father who, although he had been discharged from the hospital, was not yet strong enough to go home and was recuperating in a nursing home. I wondered how he would handle the added stress of my mother's worsening condition.

In Another World

Mom smiled when I walked into her room in the intensive care unit.

"I must look like the man from Mars," she said, self-conscious because of all the tubes running in and out of her body.

"You look beautiful to me!" I responded. But it was hard to see her so weak, and the smile on my face was betrayed by the tears that were filling my eyes.

Mom spoke immediately of her readiness to see Jesus, and I could tell that she really was at peace. But I wasn't. I wasn't ready to let go of her, and I wondered if I would be cheated of the quality time with her and my dad that I had been planning for so long.

Thankfully, over the next few days, the crisis passed and Mom began to rally. She was transferred from intensive care to the rehabilitation program, and soon she was asking the family to "spring her" from the hospital. She wanted to be home with people who loved her. She dreaded the curt, businesslike manner of the nurses who brought her medications; she protested the abrupt manner in which she was awakened in the morning to eat a breakfast that made her sick to her stomach; she resisted the intrusion of needles that left ugly, dark bruises on her thin arms and hands; she disliked the impatient scowls she received when asking for help from an overworked staff.

Of course, she understood the realities of a short-staffed hospital, but it didn't sit right with her to be treated with disregard. And she hated the condescension of being called "honey" by people who refused to address her by her name. She eventually became so frustrated that she called her brother and begged him to help her: "They slapped me in here, and now I need you to help get me out," she told him.

The doctor gave her permission to leave the next day, and when Uncle Herm came to get her that morning, she had been packed and waiting for him since 6 A.M.

With the assistance of home nursing care, she now had her heart's desire. She would be staying in the warm and comfortable environment of her younger sister's home. (Her sister is eighty.) Immediately, things took a turn for the better, and I was grateful that I had the opportunity to be part of her recovery process.

Day by day Mom began to gain strength. Her eyes, which had been so dull and lifeless, began showing new signs of life. It was so good to see a smile on her face and to hear her deliver a few one-liners that had us all laughing. I realized there was no guarantee that the recovery would be complete or long-lasting, but I promised myself that I would relish every moment we had together.

How I enjoyed our contact! When I sat on the bed next to her, Mom would look into my face and run her fingers through my hair as if I were a little girl again. It brought back memories of my grade-school years when she did my hair up in French braids. We slept together at night so I could be available in case she needed something, and that made me remember all the times I crawled in bed with her when I was a little girl so she could calm my fears. How the tables had turned. Sometimes she would reach out in the darkness to make sure I was there.

I thought a lot about the mutuality of caretaking. She buttoned my buttons and dressed me when I was a child, and now I was doing all those things for her—fixing her food, feeding her, brushing her teeth, combing her hair—doing everything I could to let her know how much I love her.

The Night of the Lost Teeth

When my brother called to let us know he was on his way for a visit, Mom was so excited she could hardly get a whisper out. Instead, she just kept repeating his name: "Donnie . . . Donnie . . . Donnie." She knew how badly it made him feel, and she hated that. But she was also anxious to see him, and we both knew he would come quickly.

About five in the morning she suddenly sat up and, in a panicked voice, asked if I knew where her teeth were. Sure enough, they were missing. I searched under the bed, under the covers, all around her, and in the bathroom, but they were nowhere to be found.

This was serious. Her son was coming to visit, and Mom needed her teeth. In the midst of her panic, I persuaded her to take a bathroom break, and that's when I saw them. She had been sitting on them the whole time. She was so happy I found them that she called me a wizard and planted a big, wet kiss on my cheek with her toothless mouth. We had a good laugh together, and when I went to turn out the small lamp on her bedside table, she said, "Keep it on till Don comes."

The next morning, as I was rushing to get her ready for Don's visit, she suddenly turned to me and said, "Judy, sit down a minute. I need you to take time with me." My cheery "good morning, get going" ritual had lacked a personal loving touch, and her feelings were hurt. I sat down next to her, put my arm around her shoulder, and apologized, "Oh, Mom, I'm so sorry for rushing you. We have all the time in the world!" We took a moment to pray together, to make a connection, and that made all the difference. What valuable lessons I was learning about love!

Don arrived just after breakfast. He was delighted to see she was doing better, and she responded to him as he cuddled her under his arm and catered to her every need. Gently, he encouraged her to take another bite of food and another small step.

As I watched them, I wondered how long it had been since we had paid her such attention. I was sad to think that it often takes a serious illness to make us get our priorities straight.

It was good to join together with my brother and sister during this family crisis, talking to Ann on the phone and spending time with Don as the three of us made important decisions about Mom's future—about the entire family's future. While going through Mom's shoe box containing an assortment of cards and handwritten notes from her children, grandchildren, and great-grandchildren, we found her note of instructions about funeral arrangements, and we all shed a few tears—tears that brought us even closer together.

A few days later, Dad was able to leave the nursing home, and the family was together for the first time in months. It seemed like "the good old days" as we sat together. Dad took Mom's hand in his while we talked about bygone days with "Do you remember?" stories.

Eventually, the discussion turned to a more serious note as I recalled my son Jeff's experience with a guardian angel the night before he died. Everyone listened attentively, in awestruck silence, for we knew we were stepping on holy ground.

"Jeff told us that he was going to die after he saw the angel," I shared. He wanted to know if it was all right with us, and Jack and I held him in our arms late into the evening to assure him of our love and God's love. He died peacefully in his sleep early that morning.

As I told the story, we all marveled together about God's grace in the midst of our pain. Over the days that followed, we were certainly going to need a special portion of that grace.

Mom began losing energy. She had no appetite. One night at supper she announced, "I don't have a bit of energy left in me. I don't want any more company."

Dad was in obvious pain as he thought about losing the woman who had been his life's partner for more than sixty years. "Maybe," he said, a hopeful note in his voice, "the Lord will come, and we'll go up to heaven together."

In the days that followed, things became worse. Mom began sleeping more and seemed to be distancing herself from the rest of the family. We often ate without her because she didn't want any food. As for me, I walked around with a queasy feeling in my stomach. I was on the verge of tears every few moments. I felt the end coming, and I was still not prepared.

On one occasion, Mom asked me if I thought Dad was ready to go on without her. I said he was getting himself ready and we cried together. "It's good to let our feelings out," she said. "Sharing tears is healing."

My extended family came to visit and sang some of her favorite hymns. What a lovely scene it was. Surrounded by her nieces and sisters, her spirits were lifted through their expressions of a common faith.

Later on, after her afternoon nap, Mom asked if I'd get some money out of her purse, go to the store, and buy us all a big steak for dinner. That's all I needed to hear. I went to the store, picked out the best-looking steak I could find, and planned our dinner. Mom had also asked for ice cream topped off with fresh strawberries for dessert. It was wonderful—amazing, really—to watch her eat every last bite of her big meal, down to the last strawberry. It was a hopeful sign.

But the next morning, when she woke up, she was disoriented and upset. "What's happening?" she asked. "What's wrong? I was cold last night, and nobody covered me up. I need help. I don't like this. I'm afraid. We have to get to the bottom of this. Why don't I get better? We've got to do something."

On and on she went, obviously in the middle of a full-blown panic attack. Nothing anyone could say or do seemed to help. Her sister, Cena, and I were shocked and dismayed by her actions. We hadn't expected anything like this. She was suspicious, fearful, and vulnerable. We did the best thing we knew to do, which was pray for Christ's presence and read the Holy Scriptures. "He who is in you is greater than he who is in the world," we reminded her. Then we played a tape of Christian music on the stereo, and that eventually seemed to calm her fears.

The next few days we seemed to be riding a roller coaster of emotions and moods—some days up and others down. One night she sat up in bed at 1 A.M. and said, "I have everything in order."

"Yes, Mom, I know you do," I responded.

Apparently reassured by my agreement that everything was, indeed, in order, she lay back down and was quickly asleep.

On another occasion she said, "I thought I was going to die this weekend. I don't know if I should let go or try harder to stay here. I know I'm in God's hands, and I trust that."

Then she surprised me with something she'd obviously been thinking about. "After I die, I'd like to leave my eyes for someone; they've been so good for me all these years." I knew how much I would love for someone to have her beautiful velvet brown eyes that had loved me so unconditionally. I'm not sure if they would accept eyes from a ninety-year-old person, but the thought that she wanted to do this touched me in a very deep place.

That night she announced, "I'd just like to go to sleep and never wake up." I knew she seriously thought that might happen, because she asked me to go through her purse to get all of her things—her checkbook, papers, and various other odds and ends—to give to my father in case her wish came true. She let me know that she had set aside her bright red blouse and white skirt to be buried in. We prayed for God's peace, and I put a Christian tape on the stereo. Actually, it was a tape that she had made years earlier when she had sung on a Christian radio station. Hearing her own voice singing of Jesus' eternal love comforted us both, and she drifted off to peaceful sleep.

The next morning, when she awoke, everything seemed different. It was as if she decided that since she hadn't died during the night, she would turn her attention to getting better. She made the announcement, "When I get better, I'll be able to walk out in the living room again." Cena and I shrugged our shoulders in puzzlement over this announcement.

We were even more amazed when she asked me to help her get dressed for the day. It was as if mother was back. She ate some cold cereal with strawberries on top, a cup of coffee with milk, and half a piece of toast. When she was finished, she gave me a big smile and said, "Boy! That tasted good!"

From that day on, Mom seemed to have a new determination to get well. She began working seriously on a plan to get stronger. Dad was doing better too, and I was encouraged to think that they would soon be back in their own home soon, living together as husband and wife. Things had taken a wonderful, unexpected turn for the better.

What a celebration we had on Mother's Day of Mom's ninety-first year! The bouquets were a bit bigger this year, the cards contained more personal notes than usual, and the phone calls that came from friends and relatives throughout the country lasted a bit longer.

We all have much to be thankful for. Our Mom is alive and doing well. Hopefully, the entire family has learned to appreciate her more. Going through this family stress has reminded each of us to take more time for love. We have grown closer and deeper as a family in our time of vulnerability.

When Time Runs Out

Loving our parents through the later stages of life is not something that comes easily. We must be willing to get emotionally involved. When we have strong bonds with our parents, we're more able to find the beauty in tending to their personal care. When there is love, we are able to admit our exhaustion and know that our parents understand. Love means we can even laugh at our mistakes and unskillful maneuvers, knowing that it is truly our intentions that matter most.

Loving our parents also demands that we be able to face their impending death. By giving them the freedom to explore what it means to them to say good-bye to this life, we empower them while, at the same time, also empowering ourselves. Through gentle openness, allowing and encouraging them to express their deepest thoughts and fears, we can help them face death with courage and dignity. By giving them permission to share their thoughts with us, we not only take in the richness of their lives, but we also gain a role model for the day when we too must say good-bye.

It's certainly not easy contemplating our parents' deaths. The death of a parent means that a significant part of your family life has come to an end. It drives home the point that yours will be the next generation in line to pass on, that someday, you too will be faced with leaving your spouse, family, and friends behind.

Most people are not comfortable talking or thinking about death, especially their own. If this is how your aging parents feel, and they don't want to talk about it, that is their right. But sometimes our own discomfort sends out a message that death is an off-limits topic. When that happens, our loved ones may refrain from talking about it, even though doing so would help them come to grips with their fears.

It is natural to fear thinking about the death of a parent. It's hard to face up to the fact that our parents are going to leave us. And it's also hard to think that someday, we too will die. Besides that, whatever fears we have about death are compounded by the fact that we live in a culture that encourages us to hide our grief and deny our mortality, thus leaving us with limited knowledge on how to deal with this stage of family life.

If you find that you are having a difficult time giving an aging parent or other family member the freedom to express his or her thoughts and concerns, you are not alone. But it is important that you find a way to overcome your fears. After all, there is no way to avoid death. It is as much a part of life as birth or growing up. It happens to every family. By embracing this stage of life rather than looking the other way or keeping the topic off-limits, we can find the deep intimacy that fills life with richness and meaning. If you need some extra assistance in this area, many local hospitals and hospices provide grief and bereavement counselors who may be able to help you.

The third chapter of Ecclesiastes reminds us that life is full of cycles and calls for us to recognize the place of each season within the grand scheme of things.

> There is a time for everything,
> and a season for every activity under heaven:
> a time to be born and a time to die, . . .
> a time to weep and a time to laugh,
> a time to mourn and a time to dance, . . .
> a time to embrace and a time to refrain.
>
> Ecclesiastes 3:1, 2, 4, 5

Just as the Bible says, a family's life cycle is full of changing seasons, of weeping and laughing, of embracing and of letting go. And within the cycles of our lives, with our pain and joy, God reveals to us but a part of the mystery of life. Happiness and sadness, triumph and tragedy are all a part of the fabric of things, and you cannot have one without the other. All are part of human experience.

It is our hope that your family will be able to eagerly embrace each season of life—for each season has its special wonder, beauty, sadness, and challenge. And as you take part in the fullness of life, know that God is always ready to lend an ear and lighten your load, eager to inspire you with energy and hope, walking alongside you every step of the way.

Time for Reflection

1. What stages of family and individual development have been most difficult for you, and why? How have you responded to those difficulties? What work remains to be done?

2. Think about how you can improve your family's communication skills. How might you communicate your wants, needs, and feelings more clearly to your spouse and/or children? How can you improve your own listening skills?

3. What rituals can your family create to celebrate various rites of passage? Ask everyone in the family to contribute ideas.

4. Are there relationships in your life that are hindering your growth and development? If so, what can you do to change them? What steps can you take if the other person is unwilling to work with you?

5. If you have lost a loved one, share with a friend, your small group, or a family member about that person's death. What do you remember? Let your feelings surface, whether they are warm, sad, angry, or funny. All of these are a part of remembering and honoring the deceased. Perhaps you will want to spend some time in a prayer of thanksgiving and remembrance for your loved one's life.

PART 3

Pain That Fractures

10

Dealing with Addiction and Divorce

The story was front-page news in the *Los Angeles Times.* Two students at the University of Southern California were found dead in their apartment, apparent victims of a heroin overdose. Both were seniors in good standing. Both came from good homes. Both had unlimited futures. But fooling around with drugs had led to an addiction neither one of them could shake. And now, that addiction had cost them their lives and left their families reeling in pain.

The story would be sad enough if it were an isolated incident, but tragically, such occurrences are anything but rare. Open your local newspaper or browse through the self-help section of any bookstore, and you can't help but be aware that many of us struggle with compulsive, addictive behaviors.

When a parent is actively engaged in an addiction and refuses to take responsibility for his or her behavior, the effects can be crippling to that person's marriage and children. Our society has even coined a phrase, "adult children of alcoholics," to describe people who are suffering from the consequences of being raised by parents who were unpredictable, abusive, or neglectful due to their addictions.

In appendix 1, we list a few good references to use if you or someone you love is struggling with an addiction. We encourage you to browse through this material, whether you are or have been actively engaged in addictive behaviors or were raised by parents who were held captive by alcoholism or drug addiction.

It is vitally important for parents who struggle with an addiction to see that there is hope and that recovery is possible, and to seek out the source of that recovery. Unfortunately, this rarely happens. Instead, most addicts go to amazing lengths to deny that they have a problem. They try to convince themselves that there really isn't any problem, or they claim that their behavior doesn't really hurt anyone, so it isn't anyone else's business. They will tell you forcefully that, "I don't have a problem. *You're* the one with the problem."

The truth is that a parent with an addiction has an important choice to make. Addictive parents can either remain stuck, letting the next fix or the next drink remain more important than their spouse, children, or family's well-being; or they can engage in the process of healing.

Remaining Stuck in Addiction

We've heard too many horror stories from people raised by parents who were too stuck in their addiction and too afraid to embrace recovery.

Julie, for example, can't remember a time when her mother didn't have a drinking problem. Her dad abandoned the family when she was just twelve, leaving her to cope with her mother on her own. Weekends when Julie's mother wasn't out in bars, she brought strange men home, many of whom were sexually abusive to Julie.

When Julie was fourteen, she attempted suicide. Although her mother was concerned, she couldn't admit to herself or anyone else that it was her own irresponsible behavior that had brought her daughter to such a low point.

When Julie was sixteen, she tried to kill herself again, and this time she nearly succeeded. In the process of her recovery, she confronted her own anger at her father for leaving and at her mother for her drinking problem. She pleaded with her mother to get help but, instead, was met with an indignant, "How dare you? I'm your mother!" She wouldn't accept any of the blame for Julie's "problems," and she had no intention of trying to find help for her own problem.

Now, as an adult, Julie remembers that when she was a girl she always felt older than she really was. The things she had seen and experienced left no room for childhood. As a child, she had always felt that she possessed a "wisdom beyond her age" and was amazed at how naive her peers could be. But as she grew older, she found herself less and less capable of operating in the adult world. She suffered from terrible times of self-doubt that bordered on self-hatred. She was emotionally unable to cope with the normal stresses and strains of young adulthood, and her relationships with men always seemed to turn into disasters.

As a child, she often felt like an adult. As an adult, she often feels like a child, adrift in a sea of mature, healthy, and capable adults, many of whom she used to think of as naive and lacking.

Such is the common fate of children of alcoholics. They feel old, yet they function like children. Adult children from chaotic homes often feel weathered and worn before they can even get out the door. But because there were so many developmental holes, they often can't cope with adult life. This is the legacy we leave our children

when we deny that our choices have a direct impact on
their lives. But it doesn't have to be this way.

Seeking Recovery and Healing

Children can heal from our mistakes if we seek reconciliation, as Robert's story attests.

Robert remembers that during much of his children's
early years, he was actively involved in alcohol and
cocaine addiction. Occasionally, Jason and Kimberly,
who were two and three years old, respectively, were in
the car with him when he made his drug deals.

Eventually, his lifestyle caught up with him, and he lost
custody of the children. Then, a nearly fatal accident
shook him to his senses. Over the past five years he has
diligently tended to his recovery. Today he is a man of
true humility, a man who possesses a wisdom born out
of coming to terms with the demons in his life. And from
the day he entered a recovery program, he has assumed
the responsibility of repairing the damage his addiction
caused his children.

It was inspiring to watch a series of family sessions in
which Robert took each of his children in his arms and
apologized to them for his mistakes. We looked on as he
told them how much he loved them and that he wanted
to be a different kind of father the rest of his life. His
openness has allowed Kimberly and Jason to share how
frightened they were at times, how much they wanted
to "make him all better," and that they often thought it
was all their fault.

As Robert calmed their fears and relieved them of the
responsibility of needing to take care of his problem, their
own anger began to surface. And Robert was able to
accept that as well. He knows that he hurt and betrayed
them and that their anger is understandable. Although it
wasn't easy, he let his children know that he wants to hear

all of their feelings, including the angry, sad, and scared ones, so they won't have to carry them around anymore.

As Robert walked with his children through this process of recovery, they learned many valuable truths. They know that adults are capable of making mistakes, but they also know now that adults can face up to their mistakes and change. They have learned that even though life is sometimes tough and unfair, we can get safely through it all—together. They have learned about humility, love, and forgiveness.

Today Robert's kids are teenagers. He has an active role in their lives, and the bonds of love are strong. It's exciting to see how assertive and confident they are— how they stand up to peer pressure with such conviction and strength. Kimberly is a peer counselor, often using her own family story as an example of hope for others who are still caught in destructive patterns.

In today's world, we understand that addictions are a disease. But we often misunderstand what that means. It does not mean that an addiction is a process that just happens to people, leaving them no choice but to be passive victims. Nothing is further from the truth. Whether or not addictions are a disease, you always have a choice. Perhaps it is true that your only initial choice is to seek medical intervention. But after that, there are many other choices ahead that can lead to recovery.

If you are caught in the grip of an addiction, there is support out there, just waiting for you to take hold of it. As the ads for Alcoholics Anonymous say, "Help is only a phone call away." Your children are waiting.

Divorced and Determined to Recover

During the past ten years, several studies have taken a close look at adult children of divorced parents to see what effect, if any, the divorce of their parents had on their lives. While some researchers maintain that divorce produces only a manageable little "blip" in the developmental life cycle of children, the overwhelming evidence is that quite the opposite is true. For example, Judith Wallerstein[8] and a group of researchers have conducted a series of in-depth studies of children of divorce. These studies spanned fifteen years, beginning with the divorce event and following these children into adulthood. The findings are sobering.

First of all, it has become apparent that watching and experiencing their parents' marriage is an essential piece of a child's development. Children learn about relationships not only by watching their mom and dad love and care for each other but also by watching them argue and resolve their differences. They learn about the ultimate expression of one's sexuality as they observe their parents romancing each other.

When we fail in our relationship with our spouse, we fail our children as well. Such failure produces a lasting impact on that part of a child's internal development which is dependent on his or her parents' relationship. This explains why children of divorce often express a pervasive fear of being disappointed, betrayed, or abandoned, even though caring and loving relationships were maintained with each parent after a divorce.

A healthy, intact marriage provides safety and a sense of identity and belonging. Safety, in turn, provides a firm ground for growth. When a marriage ruptures, the child's identity is shaken and fear creeps in, undermining his or her development. It is not surprising that children of divorce often experience difficulty in academics and social relationships. Often, a young teenager will unknowingly try to soothe the fear brought on by his or her parents' divorce by becoming sexually promiscuous or engaging in substance abuse.

As adults, children of divorce are more prone to many shallow relationships that come and go because they have not had the pattern of a loving and enduring relationship. Some children of divorced parents grow up to be worried underachievers with little belief in their abilities to succeed.

Looks like a pretty grim picture, doesn't it! To help your own children heal, to equip them with the best possible chance of not repeating your own mistakes, you must recognize that what happens in your marriage affects them.

Unfortunately, we're noticing a disturbing trend in popular literature, which is that divorce is seen as "no big deal." The breakup of marriage has become so common that we are beginning to treat it as normal. In doing that, society has tended to downplay the effects divorce has on children. The truth is that divorce does affect children, and if its effects are left unrecognized and untreated, they can and often do result in serious damage.

Of course, it's important to have a balanced view. It does no good to condemn the person who is caught up in the middle of a divorce, but neither does it help to just shrug and say, "Oh well, it happens to the best of us." It is easy to lose hope when your friends, family, or church judge and ostracize you in the midst of your pain. But in our attempts to regain hope, we may be tempted to avoid seeing the consequences our choices have had on our children.

No, divorce is not the unpardonable sin. No, divorced people should not be treated as lepers by their Christian brothers and sisters. But at the same time, divorce is not something that can be shrugged off lightly, because it does produce long-lasting, negative consequences that affect all of those touched by it. Recovery from divorce is possible, but as is true with those caught up in addictive behaviors, it is possible only when you recognize the severity of the situation and, with God's help, work toward recovery.

The consequences of divorce—and a dysfunctional marriage—on a child's development remind us that our marriage commitments are not simply for our benefit. They are intended to protect and nurture our children as well. The struggles of those who are learning to cope with parental divorce can teach us all a valuable lesson: We must tend to our marriages with diligence, not take our spouses for granted, and never assume that "our children will just learn to deal with divorce" and will move on unscathed.

Many resources currently available address recovery, and we have cited a few of them in our appendix 1. These resources explain in more detail the effects of divorce on children at various ages and give ways of working with them through the difficult time following a divorce.

Working through Addiction and Divorce

Do you have a family member who is actively engaged in an addiction or who is embroiled in severe marital discord, yet who shows no sign of taking responsibility for the situation? Do you fear for the emotional and/or physical well-being of their young children? If so, you may be asking yourself, "What can I do?"

There is no easy answer to this question, because the dynamics of each family differ, and some people refuse to change or admit their problems no matter how much you may try to help them. But still, we have three suggestions that can be applied to almost all families and situations.

1. *Talk directly with your family member about the situation.* Share your observations and concerns—especially for their children—and ask them if they

will seek help. Offer to help them find a good therapist or a local pastor. Help them find caring and capable family members or friends who can help care for the children while they are still seeking recovery. Clear, caring communication often is lacking in times of chaos. Sometimes what people in trouble need most of all is someone who cares enough to speak clearly to them about what they're doing—to point out their destructive behavior with an offer of support to help deal with it.

2. *Put together a "family intervention."* Some people who are involved in addiction or severe marital discord are often so caught up in self-destructive patterns that they are unreceptive to the encouragement of loved ones. This is where a family therapist or drug and alcohol counselor may be able to offer you some assistance in putting together an intervention.

A family intervention involves gathering family members and close friends to constructively confront the person about his or her problem. The goal is to push that person into realizing how destructive the behavior is, especially for the children involved, so that he or she will actively seek help. An intervention is also a time to affirm your love and concern for the person, and to provide avenues and resources for obtaining help.

Family interventions are most effective when they are organized and assisted by a trained family therapist or addictions counselor. These professionals know how to manage the high emotions that are often present in these meetings. They also know how to steer the interaction so that it remains productive rather than destructive. And once they are presented with the particular situation in your family, they will have an idea of how best to proceed. Of course, there are no guarantees that the outcome will be exactly what you want, but family interventions are powerful acts of love that can often bring family members to the place of seeing the situation they are in and agreeing to seek the help they need.

3. *Seek outside help to protect children who are caught up in destructive behavior.* If your family member is resistant to your other efforts, and if you suspect that her or his children are being physically and/or emotionally abused, endangered, and/or neglected, it may be necessary to seek outside help in order to protect them. Here again we recommend that you seek the advice of a competent therapist. An outside set of ears can help you determine if you are underreacting or overreacting to the situation. (After all, when you are in the middle of a crisis situation, it's easy to question your judgment.)

Some situations demand that immediate action be taken to protect vulnerable children. This might involve you or another family member seeking temporary custody of the children involved, or it might mean calling your local child protective service agency.

This reminds us of the predicament faced not long ago by a woman named Helen. Her older brother, Steve, and his wife, both of whom had a long history of drug and alcohol addiction, had recently become parents of a healthy baby boy. Unable to cope with the needs of a baby, both Steve and Brenda had resumed their addictions shortly after Jackson's birth. By the end of his first month of life, his parents barely had a sober moment. Often, Helen would visit the family, only to find the baby crying alone in his crib, hungry and dirty.

The extended family pulled together to baby-sit, feed, and care for him. At first, the couple welcomed the help. But soon, defensiveness set in, and they became angry because "everyone must think we're lousy, incompetent parents." Helen's mother had the most access to Steve, but she constantly made excuses for him, dismissing his drinking as a "tension reliever" and minimizing the danger this behavior posed to the baby. She assumed the same enabling role with her son that she had always taken with her alcoholic husband.

Soon, Helen became aware of other, more dangerous incidents. Jackson was left alone at home on numerous occasions; both parents often drove under the influence with the baby in the car, and Brenda was suffering from blackouts due to her heavy binge drinking. Various family members tried encouraging both of them to seek help. A family intervention was attempted, but neither of them worked with the process. Helen felt that the only choice left to her was to contact the child welfare office in Steve's hometown.

Helen feared that her brother and sister-in-law would hate her for the rest of her life, but she also knew that someone had to be the baby's advocate. She felt that she would have a difficult time dealing with her guilt if she did not act to respond to the little boy's pain, to protect him from life-threatening danger. She knew very well that what was happening to Jackson during his first six months of life would affect him forever if help didn't come quickly. Helen and Steve were both proof of that, having grown up in a chaotic family themselves.

Ultimately, Helen opted to have an addictions counselor file a report with Child Protective Services—the same counselor who was already familiar with the family. Because of that report, a child welfare worker went to the home, found signs of neglect, and placed Jackson in the temporary care of one of Brenda's sisters. Steve and Brenda were allowed supervised visits, with the stipulation that they both participate in treatment for alcoholism. A family therapist was assigned to the case, and it was made clear to the parents that their son would be returned to them when, and only when, they had proved they could be fit parents.

In this case, it took losing custody of their son before Steve and Brenda sought help. Luckily for Jackson and his parents, the family didn't sit and watch passively as another generation became ravaged by family chaos.

It took courage to do what Helen did, but she acted decisively, out of love for her family, based on her belief that change and healing could take place. Fortunately, she did not have to act alone but with the support of family members, friends, and therapists—and ultimately, with the assistance of an outside governmental agency. In other words, she sought out the external resources that were available to her.

We share this story because so many of us are faced with these extreme family traumas, and often nobody does anything about them because they are embarrassing and difficult to talk about, much less deal with. Oftentimes, we decide just to accept the chaos, and the situation becomes second nature to us.

But we cannot afford to ignore difficult and dangerous situations, especially if children are involved. It is primarily to protect them that decisive, courageous action must be taken. The typical challenges of day-to-day growing up are tough enough. But to live with the constant threat of family disintegration or of personal harm within one's own home—which should be a child's safe haven—not only is unbearable but is a violation of our adult responsibility toward those who are weaker and more vulnerable than we are.

Helen and Brenda's family reminds us that solutions do exist. And perhaps most encouraging of all, that we do not have to seek out these solutions alone.

11

Suicide, the Ultimate Abandonment

Her shoulders shook with convulsive sobs as she leaned forward in the chair, her face buried in her hands. It was a long moment before she was ready to resume her story. Then through her tears she said, "I knew he was depressed. But everybody gets depressed once in a while. I never thought..." She stopped a moment to swallow the lump in her throat. "I never thought he'd kill himself. Why? Why did he do it?"

Two weeks earlier, Evelyn's twenty-three-year-old son had committed suicide in his college dorm. He was a good student, two weeks away from graduation. Everyone had always thought of David as bright, capable, and generous. They all thought he'd have a great future. And now he was gone, through his own hand, and his broken-hearted mother was left to try to make some sense out of the pain and grief that was tearing at her heart. It would be a long, long time before her life would regain any semblance of normalcy.

What drives someone to take his or her own life? It's difficult to imagine the private hell that would cause someone to commit such an unthinkable act. Yet, in our society, people take their own lives every single day—thousands of them every year. And in the process, they bequeath their bereaved loved ones a legacy of overwhelming pain, sorrow, and guilt.

Survivors are left asking themselves questions like: "What could I have done to prevent this?" "Why didn't I see the signs that something was wrong?" "How could he (or she) do this to me?" There are conflicting emotions of guilt, anger, and shame.

A suicide within the family is usually stuffed into the closet with the other skeletons as quickly as possible. It is a shameful and hurtful event that is never talked about, except in a soft whisper. Everyone tries to put the pieces back together in their own private way, leaving misunderstandings that go uncorrected and eventually become part of the family myth. Generally, because of its nature, suicide is harder to deal with than other types of family tragedies.

Some years ago, our extended family members faced the suicide of one of our beloved members. Everyone tried to make sense out of something that made no sense. What we did know was that a wonderful young man who was loved by his family took his own life. The complications of dealing with his suicide were excruciating. There were unanswered questions left dangling in everyone's minds—the unknowns surrounding the circumstances of his death, the anguish of dealing with police and the media, sorting through personal items, traveling to the scene, making funeral arrangements, and the pain of grappling with the spiritual questions. Those stressors, on top of the terrible shock of losing our loved one, were almost more than any of us could bear.

Finally, the family was able to lay this dear one to rest in a private graveside ceremony. Setting aside this time to give tribute to this young man (a son, brother, grandson, nephew, uncle, and friend) became an essential part of the healing. Much of the grief work would continue over many months and years, but taking the time to remember him for the life he had lived—and not just for the way he died—was an important first step in the healing process.

His mother found that keeping a journal was a particularly helpful way for her to deal with her grief. Her young granddaughters drew pictures and used paints and colors to express their feelings. Grandparents found a sensitive book helpful. All the family members were grateful for the loving support of others.

Surviving the Suicide of a Loved One

When a member of your family chooses to end his or her life, you are traumatized in ways that differ from other types of loss. If you have been touched by suicide, it is vitally important that you work to get to the point where you can acknowledge the reality of what has happened. Ignoring the painful reality or trying to stuff it deep in a hole somewhere will only prolong the pain and worsen the trauma.

Over the next few pages, a young woman shares the feelings she experienced after her brother committed suicide. She not only speaks of what the coping process is like but tells what types of responses were most helpful for her.

"My parents and I are referred to as the 'survivors of suicide.' At the time of writing this paper, I and my parents have been survivors of my brother's suicide for eighteen months. The thing about being a survivor is that you will always be one. It does not wear off or go away with time. Often the stigma associated with suicide, especially in the Christian community, is like a huge burden to carry.

It's tempting to cover up and hide the truth instead of being open and honest about the suicide.

"Everyone in my family went through the many wrenching emotions of shock, relief, catharsis, depression, guilt, preoccupation with loss, and anger. We all did it in a different order and time frame, which means we were sometimes out of sync with each other. All these feelings are honorable, and we must be allowed to react without being judged. We needed unconditional acceptance.

"Quiet support from friends was the most helpful to me. When people listened to me, I was able to sort out my own feelings without having them jumbled up with somebody else's advice. There were many times that I just needed someone to sit quietly with me, neither one of us talking. After my brother died, a good friend and I went blueberry picking. Just to be out in the sunshine picking blueberries with my close friend was exactly what I needed.

"It was so important for people to let me react in my own way. Sometimes I did not want to be hugged, particularly at the funeral. This was my time to have private connection with my deceased brother. I also did not like being told that I should just have a good cry. . . . It doesn't help to be told what to feel.

"One of the most difficult things for me was to hear that my brother had committed a grave sin for taking his life. Questioning his salvation was offensive and extremely hurtful.

"Some people were terribly insensitive and intrusive with their many curious questions. We experienced some long-distance phone calls from people who only seemed interested in the how, when, where, and why of things. This bordered on cruelty, in my mind. My brother was dead. I had lost my dearest friend. How could they miss the point so badly?

"My deepest feelings were felt between four to six months after the suicide, just when most people think the survivor is getting on with life. My depression took me to a low place, and it was an important part of my grief. . . . One of the more difficult comments I had spoken to me was, 'You can't stop living, you know.' What a cruel stab! In order for me to go on living, I had to feel the depth of my loss.

"Those who knew my brother had their own grief to bear. Some seemed to want me to be there to help them grieve. This is the last thing a survivor is able to do—or should be expected to do. Please find your own resources so you can bring comfort when you are able to be there for the immediate family. Obviously, there is a difference between grieving with the family, expressing the loss through tears and weeping, and falling apart hysterically in such a way that forces the immediate family into caring for you.

"Cliches were totally unhelpful. I remember someone who advised, 'Cling to the promises of the Bible.' A simple, 'I'm so sorry,' means so much more.

"Those who helped the most were those who understood we were in a cloud of shock. Nothing was clear or believable, and we were in a horrifying fog. We were not able to eat because we did not realize we were hungry. My husband's boss came over and handed us a bag of deli food from the store. There were breads, meats, cheeses, salads, chips, and cookies. This was the kindest thing that was done for us. The food lasted for several days, and when it was gone, there were no dishes to return to anyone.

"Cards meant so much! You do not have to write anything. Just sign your name. It was comforting to us to open a card and see the name of one who cared. Some remembered to send a card a month after the death to let us know they were still thinking of us. This was the time when we were feeling the most pain. Also, sending a card on the anniversary of the death indicates a deep level of care and understanding. This is always a difficult day, and the extra support means so much.

"I was fortunate to have some good friends who listened to me and let me say whatever was on my mind, no matter how shocking. They walked with me through the depths of despair and on into the healing process. I was not judged or made to feel guilty for my feelings. These were the ones who continued to ask me how things were going.

"As the happiness slowly seeps back into the life of the survivor, enjoy the good days with them. I was especially grateful for those who could reminisce about the good memories of my brother.

"I close by saying that suicide is not an unforgivable sin. Do not be afraid to say the word suicide or to acknowledge that the victim took his/her own life. God is the only one who can understand the heart of the victim. Casting judgment or trying to make the suicide 'go away' is very damaging. After a suicide, it is important to give support, acceptance, compassion, and concern. By being aware, we can envelop survivors in a safe haven as they make it through the grief process. As the church of Jesus Christ, let us wholeheartedly embrace this important mission to the survivors in our families, churches, and communities."

There is so much wisdom in what she says!

When Frederick Buechner, author of *Telling Secrets,* was ten years old, his father went into the garage, started his car, and waited for the exhaust to kill him. Frederick was told that he would now have to be the "man of the family," which left a heavy burden of guilt, anger, and grief that anyone would have trouble carrying, much less a young boy.

Buechner writes: "His suicide was a secret we nonetheless tried to keep as best we could, and after a while my father himself became such a secret. There were times when he almost seemed a secret we were trying to keep from each other."

He goes on to say that he lost a father he had never really found. He quotes his character Godric, who said, "It's like a tune that ends before you've heard it out. Your whole life through you search to catch the strain, and seek the face you've lost in strangers' faces."

"I am my secrets," Buechner admits in his book, "the truth that although death ended my father, it has never ended my relationship with my father—a secret that I had never clearly understood before."

Buechner comes to the conclusion that God makes himself known powerfully and personally through the painful events of our lives. And the fact that God is mightily present in such private events does not mean to suggest that He makes the events happen.

"Instead, events happen under their own steam as random as rain, which means that God is present in them not as their cause but as the one who even in the hardest and most hair-raising of them offers us the possibility of new life and healing which I believe is what salvation is. For instance, I cannot believe that a God of love and mercy in any sense willed my father's suicide; it was my father himself who willed it as the only way out available to him from a life that for various reasons he had come to find unbearable. God did not will what happened . . . but I believe that God was present in what happened. I cannot guess how he was present with my father—I can guess much better how utterly abandoned by God my father must have felt if he thought about God at all—but my faith as well as my prayer is that he was and continues to be present with him in ways beyond my guessing. I can speak with some assurance only of how God was present in that dark time for me in the sense that I was not destroyed by it but came out of it with scars that I bear to this day, to be sure, but also somehow the wiser and stronger for it."[9]

Overcoming Pain and Grief through Ritual

We have found that a most effective way to deal with the pain and sorrow of suicide is to undertake a ritual commemorating the life of the person who has taken his or her own life. The ritual we are about to describe can be adapted to meet the needs of your particular family and situation. (It can also be used to deal with other types of family pain, such as nonsuicidal deaths, miscarriages, the inability to conceive the child you've always wanted—the pain of infertility will be discussed in the next chapter—and so on.)

Start by placing four candles on a stand. Then, with the family gathered together, say, "We light these four candles in honor of you: One for our grief. One for our courage. One for our memories (or unfulfilled memories). And one for love."

As you light the first candle say, "This first candle represents our grief. The pain of losing you is intense. It reminds us of the depth of our love for you."

As you light the second candle say, "This second candle represents our courage—to confront our sorrow, to comfort each other, to change and continue on with our lives."

As the third candle is lit, say, "The third candle is in your memory—the times we laughed, the times we cried, the times we were angry with each other, the silly, unique things you did, the caring and joy you gave us (or the hopes we had for these memories)."

In lighting the fourth candle, say, "This last candle is the light of love. We cherish the special place in our hearts that will always be reserved for you. We thank you for the gift your life brought to each of us. We love you."

A variation of this ritual is to make an arrangement of candles, each one representing a family member who is no longer living. During a holiday season, you may want to incorporate such a ritual into the time of family togetherness. You may express your thankfulness for the departed loved one(s) as you gather around the dining room table at Thanksgiving, or you may want to make an ornament for your Christmas tree with the name(s) of the deceased family member(s) lovingly displayed. As the years pass by, rituals such as these serve to remind us that our departed loved ones remain alive within our hearts, that they are present in the love we give to one another and within the sharing of common memories.

It is our hope that these ideas will inspire you and your family to find ways of celebrating the lives of those who have gone on before you.

Responding to a Suicidal Family Member

We would be remiss in talking about the pain of suicide if we neglected to spend some time talking about the best way of responding to a friend or family member who you suspect may be thinking about taking his or her own life.

The truth is that suicidal feelings creep over many of us during times of deep despair. Very few people make it through adolescence or into adulthood without occasionally thinking that death might be a better option than sticking it out. But for some people, these thoughts and feelings linger and intensify. Soon their judgment becomes clouded. They may become convinced that death really is the best way out of their problems.

Thus, suicidal feelings progress through various stages, developing from a passing thought to a well-devised plan. Different people progress through these stages at different rates, so it is important to listen carefully even to those fleeting thoughts regarding suicide. This is the stage when we are most capable of tending to the distress that is causing such pain, whether in ourselves or in those we love.

Of course, it is often hard to pick up on the suicidal cues of another. Some wish to keep their intent private. Others send mixed messages. They may say they want to die, yet what they really want is an end to their pain. The following list of suggestions is intended to provide you with ways of responding when you suspect that a friend or family member might be thinking about suicide.

1. Do not feel that you are responsible for solving all of this person's problems. The pain may be deep and the situation such that it requires extensive professional help. It is not so important that you know "the right thing" to say or do. It is important that you express your love, care, and concern.
2. If you notice a marked change in someone's behavior—if he appears to be depressed, agitated, or withdrawn in some way that suggests he is having trouble coping with life—simply ask him how he is doing, if anything is bothering him, and let him know you're interested in what he's thinking and feeling.
3. If someone has expressed thoughts or feelings of wanting to hurt or kill herself, ask her to tell you more. Give her permission to talk about it. It is the things we keep secret that hold the most power over us.
4. Even if the suicidal thoughts and feelings (called suicidal ideations) are fleeting, suggest that he talk with a counselor. Ask him if he knows of a therapist he can talk with; if he doesn't, offer to help him find one.
5. If someone is expressing clear statements about wanting to "go away" or die, speak up immediately. Contact another family member, a friend, a teacher,

a coworker, or an employer, and tell them you suspect this person might be suicidal.

6. If you fear for this person's immediate safety, call
911 or the emergency telephone number in your
area. Most hospitals and police or fire departments
have suicide assessment teams. These are trained
mental health professionals who will come to that
person's home, where they will determine if safety
precautions are necessary. It is not your job to
determine whether your fear is valid! If you suspect
someone is in danger, let the assessment team figure out whether more assistance is needed.

7. Remember that all feelings go through cycles. Generally, intense suicidal feelings will pass in time if
the person involved receives some help. If your
friend or family member is indeed suicidal, he or she
will need constant supervision for the next forty-
eight to seventy-two hours, at least. If an assessment
team determines that this person is in imminent
danger of self-destruction, he or she will be placed
in supervised medical care for a specified number
of days, depending on the regulations of your state.
While this hospitalization may be against everyone's
wishes, especially the suicidal person's, it may be
the only way to keep your loved one alive.

8. Be prepared for the response you're going to get
from the person you're trying to help. Some may
want medical intervention. Others may be furious
that you interfered. Some will appreciate your care,
while others may resent you and even go so far as
to terminate contact with you. If this happens,
remember that a person who is contemplating suicide is already upset with life. Thinking and deci-
sion-making capabilities have become temporarily
distorted. Your job is not to please this person, but
to keep him or her safe.

9. Be warned that responding to a suicidal person is exhausting. It will tax your own reserves, so make sure you are taking care of yourself too. Talk with a supportive family member or friend about what happened and what it was like for you—whether it was scary, difficult, or aggravating. Then do something energizing! Physical exercise is a great way to shake off tension. Or if you feel exhausted, take a long nap. Perhaps it will help you to pause for awhile to meditate on your own appreciation for life, your thankfulness for all the blessings God has given you, for your awareness of God's presence in your life even during the tough times.

A Cry for Help

When a person chooses to kill himself, we know the pain must have become so overwhelming that he could no longer hold on to the hope that solutions exist, that things can get better tomorrow, or that his life could once again have meaning and purpose. Each person arrives at the brink of suicide for different reasons, but all have in common the inability or reluctance to rely on the internal and external resources that would help pull them through a time of trouble.

Yes, some—though not all—suicide victims were never able to develop adequate coping resources during childhood due to turbulent family relationships. If you saw the movie *Dead Poets Society,* you remember the story of the teenager who took his own life. Unable to tolerate the extremely high and rigid expectations placed on him by his father, the boy falsely believed that the only way he could find peace and freedom was through death. He couldn't see beyond the moment, that other options existed; so he killed himself precisely because he wanted life. He could not find any other way to cope. Tragically, such scenes are commonly played out in real life.

Yet not all people who attempt suicide are fully intent on dying. That's the primary reason why suicide attempts outnumber actual suicides by a ratio of ten to one. Most often there is a sense of ambiguity for people caught in the depths of despair. They cannot decide between death and life, so many suicide attempts are actually desperate pleas for help.

Many persons who attempt suicide can, after receiving help, move on and continue with a satisfying life. The actual crisis period may be brief in duration.

You Are Not Guilty

Please remember that you, alone, are not responsible for preventing someone you love from committing suicide. You cannot read anyone's mind, and the person who is contemplating taking his or her life is not likely to tell you plainly, "I am going to kill myself." If you didn't see the signs at the time but see now that perhaps you could have done something to prevent the suicide, please remember that you are not responsible for what someone else may do.

Still, when a family member commits suicide, the unanswered questions can be haunting:

How could I have missed the warning signs?
Why didn't I get more involved?
Could I have prevented it by being a better friend (or parent, child, sibling, or spouse)?

You may be haunted by memories of your last conversation with the suicide victim, wondering if you could have said something that would have prevented it—or, even worse, if you said something mean or insensitive that pushed her over the edge. You may be left thinking, "If she really loved me (or the family) she wouldn't have done this to us."

The answers to some of these questions may be disturbing. Yes, there may have been signs that you didn't see. Deepening depression; a sudden, unexplainable lift from a depression; increasing moodiness; risk-taking behavior; spending time getting one's affairs in order; distancing oneself from the rest of the family; or suddenly becoming very expressive with regard to one's love and concern for the family—all of these may be signs that someone is contemplating taking his own life.

Sometimes there are masked messages, such as, "Sometimes I wonder if I'm going to pull through this." Other times, the messages are more to the point, as in "I wish I were dead" or "I want to die."

As this list of possible signals illustrates, the signs are not always clear or their meaning apparent. While we may all need to learn how to be more attentive to what our loved ones are experiencing, we cannot always discern the scribbles on the wall. And again, please remember that if the tragic shadow of suicide should fall across your family, *you are not responsible.*

You may see ways you failed the person who took his or her life. All of us, though, fail our family and friends in some way or another. Failure is simply part of human nature, of our experience here on this fallen planet. Yes, we share in the responsibility for the pain our behavior causes in those we abuse, neglect, or take advantage of. Still, the only choices we can take responsibility for are the choices we make.

You are responsible for how you respond to the pain in your life, but you cannot take responsibility for someone else's choices. Sometimes, the only lesson we can learn from a loved one's suicide is to never take our relationships with others, or our own life, for granted.

12

The Pain of the Child You Never Had

It was the day of the company picnic—a day when all the employees brought their spouses and children to the park for food, games, pony rides, and all types of family fun. Everyone was having a great time. Everyone, that is, except Rhonda, who sat all alone, wearing a pained expression and occasionally dabbing at her eyes with a handkerchief. Rhonda—thirtyish, pretty, and vivacious— was usually the life of any social gathering. But not today. Definitely not today!

When Donna saw the state her friend was in, she walked over, sat down beside her, and put her arm around her.

"You okay?" she asked sympathetically.

"No," Rhonda sobbed. "I'm not okay. I knew I shouldn't have come. Seeing all these families with their children . . . it's just too hard to take."

Donna didn't know what to say, so she just sat there, letting Rhonda know how much she cared. She knew that Rhonda and her husband had been married for nearly ten years and had always looked forward to having a house full of children. But when after two years of marriage nothing had happened, a trip to a specialist confirmed their worst fears. Rhonda was never going to be able to have any children of her own.

Most of the time, Rhonda was able to hide her pain behind her quick wit and friendly smile. Because she had no children of her own, she lavished attention and presents on her nieces and nephews. But deep inside, the pain gnawed away at her heart, and it would not go away. And today, seeing the happy families playing together—the mothers, fathers, and their children—was breaking her heart. Rhonda could tell you that infertility is one of the most painful realities a married couple can face.

Infertility is described as a condition in which a couple cannot conceive a child despite consistent attempts for at least one year. Impairment may involve either the man's or the woman's reproductive system, but it is often a combination of both. While many infertile couples eventually conceive, usually with medical intervention, a large percentage of infertile couples find out they are sterile—which is what happened to Rhonda and her husband—a condition defined as a permanent inability to have biological children.

For a variety of reasons, more and more couples are having increased difficulty conceiving. Some couples put off having a family to concentrate on their careers or for other reasons, only to find out they have waited too long. But that is only one reason for increasing infertility rates. Some suspect that living in a much more polluted and stressful environment is taking its toll on many people's reproductive systems.

Whatever the cause of infertility may be, when a couple cannot have children, often the first thing their family and friends want to know is why—which inevitably means, Which one of you has the problem? While this may be a normal response, it generally adds to the pain of a couple that is already in a time of crisis. It doesn't really matter who has the problem. Infertility is a condition that engulfs both partners in a marriage. It causes pain for both husband and wife, and dealing successfully with the situation requires mutual cooperation and support.

Infertility and sterility are not just medical conditions. For most couples, this may be the toughest emotional and relational challenge of their lives.

The Losses of Infertility

Not being able to have children can set in motion a complex web of losses. Being a parent enables us to fully pour our time and energy into the care of another, to give to another the love that was given to us. Going back to chapter 5, you may recall Erikson's stage of generativity. Parenting is about giving to this world in a meaningful and lasting way by raising another human being who, in turn, will love and contribute as well. It is one of the most rewarding ways to pass on the wisdom and beauty of life that we have experienced. Having children not only leaves a genetic piece of you behind but also allows you to represent in bodily form your love and union with your spouse. It also allows you to keep the memory of your ancestors alive in physical form.

Rhonda says that she never really needed to see herself "genetically reproduced," but the worst part of her sterility was the knowledge that she would never see her husband's mannerisms in her children, nor would she ever be able to see glimpses of her parents and grandparents in her children's smiles. In each of her nephews and nieces, she sees bits and pieces of her ancestors; but she grieves that her own children, should she and her husband decide to adopt, will carry none of these traits.

Yes, most of us understand that biological ties alone do not make a family. Rather, a family is born out of commitment, unconditional love, and shared history. But the concerns highlighted above are the lost hopes and dreams that a sterile couple must grieve if they are to move on and pursue other options, such as adoption.

Let's look at some of the other specific losses experienced by the infertile couple.

1. *The infertile couple often experiences a loss of intimacy.* Many infertile couples report feelings of great sadness that their lovemaking is not capable of bringing a new life into being. For most infertile couples, intercourse has been stripped of its spontaneity, since they must instead conform to rigid schedules as to when they can and cannot have sex. Blanca recalls how, after months of trying, she and her husband Manuel admitted that they no longer even enjoyed being intimate, since it represented one more occasion of having to practice perfect timing and technique—one more stretch of time when hopes would be heightened, only to be dashed again with the start of her menstrual cycle.

2. *Infertile couples experience the loss of being able to experience the prenatal and birthing process.* It is a great loss for a woman not to be able to experience the wonderment of life growing within her body. Most women have heard numerous accounts and perspectives regarding what it's like to carry a child, but what is remembered most by those who cannot have children are the stories told by those who loved every minute of pregnancy. They recall hearing women talk of how much they enjoyed watching their bodies change, sensing movement for the first time, tuning in to their unborn child's sleep and wake cycles, and so on.

   An infertile woman has a heightened awareness that her body will never be able to fully realize one of its prime functions. Since she was a teenager, the infertile woman has been aware of her body's cycles, month after month preparing itself to harbor new life. As her breasts developed, she wondered what it would be like to sustain life with nourishment that would flow from her own body. All of these hopes and dreams are taken away when a husband and wife cannot have children of their own.

3. *Infertile couples sometimes suffer the pain of miscarriage.* Tragically, it is an all-too-common experience for many couples seeking infertility treatment to suffer the loss of a child through miscarriage. After miraculously being able to conceive, for one reason or another the baby cannot survive in the womb and dies. This is the cruelest sort of pain—to have your hopes seem to be on the verge of being fulfilled only to have them suddenly dashed. Stories told by people who have been through such an experience are truly heartbreaking.

4. *Infertile couples may experience the loss of social relationships.* The infertile couple is often overwhelmed by the sense of isolation they feel. With each passing holiday, they notice that it continues to be just the two of them sitting at their dinner table. They wake up to an overwhelming silence on Christmas morning, aware that only gifts for each other lie beneath their tree.

Many times, the infertile couple will be treated by their friends and family members as naive youngsters, as if having children is the only way their adulthood could possibly be validated. And often, a special bonding takes place between people who have children of about the same age. The childless couple may rightly feel left out, may even find that they have gradually been squeezed out of their circle of friends.

5. *The infertile couple may feel that they have failed in a personal way.* It's vitally important for the couple that cannot conceive to realize that they have no control over the situation, that they have not failed. When negative feelings and beliefs creep into the life of the infertile couple, they must be dealt with before they become overwhelming. If such beliefs are left unattended, the nature of the problem will become distorted, and the stress of infertility will be compounded.

How do you respond to friends and family members who cannot have children? Often, it's difficult to know how to act around them. Do you avoid talking about your own kids? Do you try to avoid the subject of children altogether? When there is a childless couple in your midst, you might even find yourself wondering what else to talk about.

The best thing you can do to love such a couple through a difficult time is to simply ask them how they're doing and how you might be an encouragement to them. Remember that each couple approaches their problems differently. So simply letting them know that you love and care for them is the best place to start.

For the couple that wants children but can't have them, the intensity of the grieving is likely to ebb and flow. Each of the partners will respond in unique ways and with his or her own timing. Some infertile couples love to be surrounded by children, whereas others find that much too painful.

Most couples find that what helps them most is to have others who are willing to listen, to ask what they are thinking, and to ask how they need support from others. The caring response of friends and family members can go a long way toward helping the infertile couple cope with the pain and loss they feel.

Coping with the Losses of Infertility

How can you cope with the loss created by childlessness?

If you are dealing with the loss of infertility, you must come to see your own worth and value as being separate and apart from being a parent. Some people long to have children for the wrong reason. They want to fill a void in their lives rather than give from the strengths they possess. When those are the subconscious motives for becoming a parent, infertility can force you to confront your true inner needs and tend to them responsibly. In this way, it can be an impetus for growth.

Not being able to have children may leave you feeling as if you have plenty of love to give but don't have anyone to give it to. Because of that, there may be the temptation to believe that your life really doesn't count for much—but that's not true. That's why it is so important to broaden your perspective by examining other avenues for being generative. For some, that means adoption. For others, it may mean dedicating themselves to a charity or becoming foster parents.

As an infertile couple, you do not have a choice concerning the limitations of your body. But you do have a choice in how you respond to those limitations. This is a life-cycle challenge that will alter the course of your individual, marital, and family life forever.

Despite the pain, roadblocks, and uncertainties, many empowering options exist. You may not be able to have biological children, but nothing can take away your right, and your responsibility, to give to this world in meaningful ways.

Most important, know that you have an advocate in Jesus Christ and that you can turn to him with any thought, feeling, or heartache. Jesus is no stranger to loss and pain, and he wants to show you the way through your own pain and loss. Through God's Word, perhaps through this book, through your own prayer and meditation, and/or through the love and care of others, you can come to a place of peace and resolution.

Time for Reflection

1. If you grew up in an addictive or chaotic home, consider how this impacted your family of origin and your own development. How and why have you chosen to do things differently with your own family?

2. If you are involved in an addiction, think of someone in your life who cares about you, whom you could talk to about your situation. Remember that, no matter what you've done, God loves you and is ready to give you the courage and the ability to ask for and receive the help you need.

3. If you have been involved in a bitter divorce, or if you and your spouse have had an ongoing bitter marriage, what steps can you take to bring peace to your family?

4. Pull out your genogram and observe the events and relationship patterns in your family of origin. Describe events in your life where you experienced or witnessed any of the following incidents as a child or teenager: family secrets; death of a parent or other family member; parental discord, divorce or abandonment; economic hardship; an alcoholic or drug-addicted parent; emotional, physical, or sexual abuse.

5. If you experienced painful events as a child or teenager, how might you be displaying the effects of those events in your life today? What patterns are you repeating? What internal thoughts and feelings reveal lingering pain? How can you deal with that pain?

6. Do you find building friendships or dealing with coworkers and authority figures difficult? If so, how might your past be influencing you in these relationships?

7. How do you respond to the concept of taking responsibility for your present choices and actions? What does that mean to you? How might that be difficult? How have you already taken responsibility for your past? How have you already taken steps to break destructive patterns and create new behaviors in the present? How do you think this will empower your family?

PART 4

Dealing with
Traumatic Loss

13

Living in a Violent World Full of Pain

On Wednesday, April 19, 1995, at 9:02 A.M., a bomb exploded in front of the Alfred P. Murrah Federal Building in downtown Oklahoma City. The blast killed more than one hundred people and injured hundreds more. It sent the entire nation reeling, searching for answers as to how this could have happened. What kind of human being would perpetrate such violence against innocent children and adults?

Those who lost family members and friends will be grieving for a long, long time. Too many can only cling to photos, clothing, and other mementos of loved ones who were senselessly killed, totally without warning, on a spring day when life seemed to be so full of new and bright possibilities.

The Oklahoma City bombing was a tragedy of gigantic proportions. Sadly, though, similar sorts of tragedies, albeit on a much smaller scale, happen daily. Every day dozens of people in our country are rocked by senseless acts of violence—people are murdered, raped, robbed, mugged, run down by drunk drivers, caught in gang violence, and abused and battered in a variety of other ways. When we hear of such incidents, many of us have the feeling that "that could never happen to me—or someone I love." But then a bomb blast shatters a calm morning in the nation's heartland, and we are jolted out of our false belief that the world in which we live is safe and predictable. Yes, violence is all around us. From the moment Cain killed Abel, fallen humanity has displayed a great inclination toward violence and inflicting pain on others.

Dealing with the Pain of Sexual Violence

It is estimated that one out of every three to four women and one out of every five to six men will be, or have been, victims of sexual exploitation or assault. This figure involves both child sexual abuse, rape, and date rape.

If someone breaks into your house or steals your car, it is natural to feel personally violated. But sexual crimes differ from other crimes of violence in that the nature of these crimes involves that part of ourselves which enables us to experience intimacy at its deepest level in a caring, loving, safe, and pleasurable environment. The perpetrator of such an assault, whether seeking revenge, control, or some distorted notion of closeness, strikes at the very core of our being.

As a result, the injuries are more than just bruises. Fear and distrust, which are typical side effects of all forms of violence, are often more pronounced. Not only does the survivor of such a crime distrust the basic safety of his or her world, but close friends, family members, and spouses may be kept at arm's length as well.

Feelings of shame and guilt further complicate recovery. If someone steals your car, you can easily express your righteous indignation, stomping your feet and yelling, "Someone stole my car!" But because sexual crimes involve violence against your innermost being, you are likely to feel a sense of shame that causes you to hide, to be too embarrassed and ashamed to tell others what happened. Ironically, it is in telling others about what happened that you can begin to break the perpetrator's hold on you.

Rape, which affects both children and adults, is one of the most violent forms of sexual abuse. Nothing can prepare us for the shocking news that a family member has been sexually assaulted. The dread that grips you when your phone rings at four in the morning is indescribable. That's the way it was for Joe and Isabelle. Joe fumbled for a few moments in the darkness for the telephone before he managed to find it. When he did, he was greeted by the voice of a policeman telling him that his beautiful twenty-two-year-old daughter was in the hospital after being brutally raped.

Shock, anguish, and rage are what Joe and Isabelle felt as they listened to the gory details. After her late shift at a local restaurant, Maria had been followed home by a young man who dragged her from her car, threw her in the back seat of his car, and raped her. After that, he terrorized her for several more hours, raped her again, and then dumped her out in the street like a bag of garbage. Her life was spared, but she would never be the same again. Her innocence was lost, her freedom was lost, her beautiful smile was lost, her belief in others was lost, her emotional healthiness was lost—and on and on we could go, recounting all the damage that was done to her.

Does this rapist have any idea how many people he harmed? Does he have any remorse about what he put this young woman and her family through? Does he care about the impact his behavior has had on this woman's extended family and her community?

Such terrible news put the entire family in a state of shock. They went through the motions, doing what needed to be done to "handle" the emergency, almost in an autopilot mode. But when the full impact of the event hit, the defenses crumbled and a myriad of emotions came tumbling down like the walls of Jericho. Everyone was devastated that such a terrible thing could have happened to someone they love. The pain of rape, like all pain resulting from acts of violence, is a pain so big that we do an injustice to try to explain or describe it.

Maria's sister-in-law says, "I have murderous thoughts toward this rapist; I want to strangle him with my own two hands. I want to make sure he knows the evil he has done. It makes me angry at every man I see, and I ask myself why they don't do something to stop their own gender from doing these outrageous acts against women!"

Unfortunately, rape is not the only form of sexual abuse. Many families have been devastated when they have learned that their child has been sexually abused by a neighbor, friend, or family member.

A few years ago, a couple named Fred and Belynda decided to seek help for their teenage daughter, who had become increasingly depressed over a period of several months. Tamara reluctantly came to therapy, feeling as if she didn't have much of a choice. Gradually, she began to see that her therapist really did care about her and wanted to help her.

One day she revealed a painful secret she had harbored for years: When she was four years old, her mother's father began sexually abusing her. When she was twelve, and her grandfather had grown weaker, she finally felt strong enough to avoid contact with him. Relieved that the abuse had stopped, she just assumed that now she could get on with her life. But instead of feeling better, she found that she felt worse as time went on; the pain just became more intense. Now, at the age of fifteen, Tamara was using alcohol to numb her pain and found herself engaging in superficial sexual relations with boyfriends "in order to gain their love and acceptance."

Sadly, victims of sexual violence often believe they can handle the problem on their own and that time will heal the pain. That is far from the truth. Isolation only causes the wounds to go underground, festering and mutating into something that becomes more difficult to manage as time goes by. Many choose ways of coping that only add to their pain, turning to alcohol and other mind-numbing drugs or engaging in sexual promiscuity.

But Tamara and Maria learned that it is only by joining together with family members and friends, and making use of supportive resources such as counselors and recovery groups, that victims of such crimes can begin to mend, can find meaning and purpose in life once again.

It's not possible to turn back the clock. Innocence lost can never be regained. These two young women, and the thousands of other men and women who have been sexually victimized, know that they will never forget what happened to them, and these memories may always cause them distress. But the painful reminders that may always linger with them do not have to rob them of all of the joys of life. It is possible to rediscover that the world is full of trustworthy, loving, and caring people. And as the victim of sexual violence actively and diligently engages in the painful process of healing, she or he will experience God's grace.

If you have been touched by such violence, know that as God breaks loose the chains that bind, you will overcome the evil that has touched your life. As you work on your recovery, you are claiming Christ's healing power to restore your sense of self-worth and to reclaim your sexual wholeness amidst a world full of sexual brokenness.

Dealing with the Pain and Loss of Homicide

The story was in this morning's paper. A thirty-five-year-old mother of two, crossing a street in South Central Los Angeles while holding her six-year-old daughter's hand, was cut down by gang violence. The bullets weren't intended for her, but she just happened to be in the way.

Nothing can bring her back. She is dead, her husband is a widower, and her two young children will never again know the comfort of their mother's arms.

Today there is outrage in the city of Los Angeles over the shooting. But by next week, it will probably be forgotten, as the name of the next victim is added to the list of those who have been cut down by the random violence that plagues our society.

Most of us have almost become numb to such reports of violence. We don't want to read or hear all the terrible details, so we turn quickly to the sports page or flip over to The Shopping Channel. Yet, every once in awhile, the reality of the tragedy penetrates the walls we have tried to put around us—walls constructed to keep us from going crazy from the pain of it all.

One day, we saw a newscaster break down and cry as she reported the death of a young child who had been kidnapped from her back yard. During the newscast, that woman had reeled off a list of tragedies, seemingly without blinking an eye. But when she got to the story of that little girl, she could contain herself no longer. Her voice broke, and a tear trickled down her cheek. When that happened, the little girl became more than just a statistic. Instead, everyone watching that newscast suddenly saw her as someone who was loved and cherished but who was brutally stolen from her family.

Tragically, the pain of loss through homicide is a crushing reality that family and friends cannot escape. Within moments, in an act of senseless violence, the life of someone you love is taken. How is it ever possible to cope with something so terrible?

When such a horrible act strikes your family, it would be difficult to cope without a deep faith in God as well as the comfort and support of caring friends and other members of your family. And again, in a tragedy of this type, it is so important to make use of the resources that are available to you, such as counselors, pastors, and support groups for those who have lost loved ones to violent crimes.

A. James Van Vugt, a friend of ours shares his family's story.

"The telephone call we hope will never come interrupted the night of January 21. It was our daughter, calling long-distance to tell us that our son, Matthew, was dead from multiple gunshot wounds incurred during a robbery at the convenience store where he worked the night shift.

"Shock, grief, and disbelief rushed over us. There was no mistake. The investigating detective and the E.R. physician had confirmed that our healthy, twenty-two-year-old son was dead. Earlier that day he had called to tell me he was planning to get a safer job.

"As my heart broke with anguish, my mind turned to the words of another grief-stricken father, King David. Upon learning that his rebellious son Absalom had met a tragic death, the king was moved to tears, crying, 'O my son Absalom! My son, my son Absalom!' (2 Samuel 18:33).

"Earlier in his life, King David had wept for another son, the child of his relationship with Bathsheba. When their child died, he ceased his fasting and weeping and said, 'Can I bring him back again? I will go to him, but he will not return to me' (2 Samuel 12:23).

"I knew that I needed God's help to forgive the assailant. There was no room in my grief for anger, bitterness, and revenge. If Matthew's death was to have dignity, and if healing was to occur, I needed to turn that over to God and the justice system. Immediately, I released the *why* question. It was in the hands of a wise God. I would go to my son some day, and it would all be made plain to me then. The more necessary question was, How can we measure Matthew's life? By what yardstick would God, his loving heavenly Father, evaluate him, and how could we, as his family and friends, remember him best?

"The last eight years had not been easy with this special adopted child, who had come from Korea to join our family. His arrival in 1975, at age three and a half, had brought a great joy. He was a sweet child—obedient, polite, and affectionate. He immediately became the 'darling little mascot' at the retirement center where I was the administrator. Each Sunday he wore his favorite blue felt cowboy hat and assisted the residents as they got on and off the shuttle bus to and from church.

"The memories of happy times and of his generosity helped the healing process. Like the time shortly after he arrived from Korea, when we traveled almost eight hours by car from Chicago to a favorite cabin on the North Shore of Lake Superior. We had all been so excited to go back to a special place. After we got there, he looked around a bit, then came up to me and said, 'After supper, let's go home, okay Aboji?' He had already found some sense of security in home, and he had used the Korean word for *daddy*. If only those warm times had been forever!

"We had thought a trip back to Korea at age thirteen would perhaps answer his questions about his own identity. He enjoyed the trip, but it seemed to trigger a difficult adolescent struggle that lasted more than six years and caused a great deal of stress and grief for all of us.

"Finally, he had moved hundreds of miles away, winding up in Shreveport, Louisiana. Two years away from

Mom and Dad and one year with almost no contact, even with his very special sister, Amy.

"It's so hard for a parent to accept the need for total independence. Only a month earlier he had made an excuse not to accept the plane ticket to come and join the family for Christmas back in Minneapolis. He still wasn't ready. He hadn't proved himself. He didn't think he had earned his way back.

"The anguish of loss seems to thrive on guilt. If only we had written or called more often. Was 'tough love' really the answer to help him stand on his own feet and to be accountable for the financial and legal mess his immaturity had caused?

"The next thirty-six hours were incredible, as we traveled to Shreveport and there were able to learn the true measure of Matthew's life. Young people came all night, all day, the next night and day. The memorial service at the local church where Matthew had visited a few times was filled. The entire night shift of the Shreveport police department attended in uniform to honor him. The receiving line was full of strangers to us but many, many people who had been touched by his life in that brief time of less than two years. Customers of the convenience store, waiters and waitresses of the restaurant where he worked his second full-time job. Friends of friends who knew Matt.

"We met a girl who had been ready to drop out of school until Matt found her a tutor and encouraged her to stay. We met a man who was despairing in a dead-end, low-paying job but who had gone to trade school at Matt's insistence and was now half finished with a draftsman course. We met a young Chinese premed student, befriended by Matt when he had started working at the restaurant, who told us no one else would speak to him.

"We heard about the young single mother of two children who had been facing eviction, and how Matt had given her the $257 she needed to pay her rent.

"The beautiful flowers left at the convenience store with an unsigned note which read, 'We miss you, Matt,' conveyed someone's deep affection and sorrow. To see strong policemen weep when they told us what a fine son we had not only tore at our hearts but gave us a tremendous sense of pride. To have Matt's favorite policeman come to the house with his wife to visit with us after the service was a tribute we will cherish.

"How to measure his life? The cup was full and running over. Matt had found himself through friendship and caring for others. As we looked back at the early progress reports during the two-year period while we were waiting for the adoption to go through, each one underscored this—Matt looking out for other children, Matt comforting the ones who were crying, Matt sharing the toys we had sent, Matt looking after the ones who couldn't look out for themselves. Perhaps in our desire to measure Matt by some of the yardsticks we had imposed on our own lives, we had missed what was there all along.

"I was truly humbled. I had to ask myself, if I stripped away the degrees, the prominent position, the houses and things, the retirement fund, would my life have the value of my son's life? Have I used my talents like he did? In his brief twenty-two years, I am sure he earned double the talents entrusted to him. 'Well done, good and faithful servant.'

"Matt had found the right environment for his own discovery of self, for the use of his gifts without expectation of receiving back. He had reached a turning point in his life. Could he have accomplished much more? He was ready to meet the true loving Father he needed—and he didn't go empty-handed.

"Oh, Matt, my son. I love you, and I am so very proud of you.

"Matt, my son, my son!"

It may help you, in a time of loss, to remember that God knows exactly how you feel. After all, God's only begotten Son was murdered too.

In his account of the crucifixion, Matthew conveys the anguish Jesus felt in his darkest hour of being alone: "About the ninth hour Jesus cried out in a loud voice . . .'My God, my God, why have you forsaken me?'" (Matthew 27:46).

Throughout the Bible, we read about God's pain and anguish for our suffering. Over the centuries, God as our Parent has watched his children suffer and die. But now the Son of God was about to take all of our pain upon himself. In the garden before his crucifixion, we see Jesus sweating drops of blood, overwhelmed not only with his own impending death and separation from God but by the pain of all humanity, which he felt so keenly. Through Jesus' tears, we gain but a glimpse into the severe pain experienced by God, who had to endure the murder of his only begotten Son.

To lose a son or daughter to murder is probably the most painful event any parent can be asked to endure. Through remembering God's response to our pain, and through the stories of others who have managed to find their way through the sorrow, we find ultimate comfort in our Creator God who understands us, who walks in our shoes, and who provides us with healing and direction.

When the World Itself Is Violent

Violent loss is not always the result of man against man. Sometimes such loss occurs simply because we live in a fallen world, where things are not the way God intended them to be. So we have earthquakes, tornadoes, hurricanes, floods, fires, and other natural disasters that claim thousands of lives every year.

Destructive acts of nature often kill hundreds or thousands of people in one awful moment, wiping out entire communities in a single blow. Oftentimes, the real disaster takes place only after the destructive event ends. Those who have escaped the initial punch often face a myriad of other crises—homelessness, exposure to the elements, disease, etc.

A woman named Candace describes the eighteen-month-long ordeal she and her family endured when a wildfire ravaged their community. The family was enjoying a peaceful day at home, when they were suddenly jolted to attention by a frantic pounding on the front door. When Candace opened it, she was confronted by a weary firefighter, dressed completely in battle gear, who told her that she and her family had less than five minutes to grab whatever they could and flee for their lives. A fast-moving firestorm was heading their way, and they had no time to delay.

"A firestorm?" she thought. "How can that be true?" There wasn't even a hint of smoke in the air; the sky was blue, and the day seemed peaceful and quiet.

The firefighter hurried off to warn the neighbors, and Candace flicked on the television set to see if there was any news about this supposed firestorm. She was shocked by the scene that greeted her. Their community was being overtaken by a fire that was advancing so fast, with heat so intense, that homes seemed to be exploding in the face of it.

What should they do? Realizing there was no time to grab much of anything—except the family cat, Molly—Candace and her two teenagers dashed out to the car. Almost immediately, they noticed a distinct change in the air. The wind had picked up, and they could see a wall of flames rushing toward their property. They drove off, barely ahead of the fire. Fifteen minutes later, their home was little more than a pile of ashes.

For the next year and a half, this family of three lived in a one-bedroom apartment while they endured an endless maze of governmental procedures and red tape that prevented them from rebuilding. Not only did they have limited financial reserves with which to rebuild but limited coping resources as well. In a matter of minutes they had lost everything they owned, including the memories those possessions represented. The night table that had belonged to Candace's grandmother was gone, as was the dining room hutch that had been passed down from her father's side of the family. All the pictures and videos of her children's growing up years were gone. Favorite books and hobbies were wiped out. So was the collection of Christmas ornaments the kids had made, along with the ceramic eggs that had always been a part of their Easters together. The familiar sights, sounds, and smells of home had all gone up in smoke.

The history the family had built together, as represented through physical possessions, was gone. With every day that passed, and with every passing season, this family was forced not only to pick up the pieces of their external lives but also to confront the lingering psychological impact of their losses.

As with any crisis, families who are hit by a natural disaster enter a period of grieving. But due to the ongoing set of crises that are usually precipitated by such a disaster, the coping process presents a unique set of challenges. Generally, there are four phases of disaster recovery.[10]

1. *The heroic phase.* Generally, when a disaster strikes, people respond with heroic actions intended to save lives and property. With adrenaline pumping through their veins, some people have performed amazing feats of strength and selfless acts of courage in times of emergency.

When the Northridge earthquake hit Southern California several years ago, the entire community seemed to come together in a heroic fashion. Within minutes of the quake, neighbors were knocking on each other's doors, checking to see if anyone was injured or needed help. People who barely said hello to one another before the quake were now putting their own needs aside to look for ways to help their neighbors. This too is part of the heroic phase.

Depending on the nature of the disaster, this phase can last anywhere from a few hours to a week or more. During this time, emotional responses are strong and active. Fear prompts us to act persistently and decisively.

2. *The honeymoon phase.* The relief of having survived a catastrophic event ushers in a feeling of euphoria that usually begins a few days after the event and may last for as long as six months. With an influx of assistance on the part of the government and other agencies, there is an optimistic feeling that everything will soon be back to normal. Community support services, ranging from the Red Cross to newly formed response groups such as community shelters and information centers are external resources that are heavily relied on during this time.

In the wake of a disaster, a strong sense of community naturally develops. It seems that everyone is pulling together, and an aura of general good-feeling covers everything despite the losses that have been incurred. But then, as time goes by and things aren't getting back to normal quite as fast as expected, the third phase sets in.

3. *The disillusionment phase.* As we see public interest in our predicament lessening and some families receiving adequate support while others receive almost nothing, hope is gradually replaced with strong feelings of disappointment, anger, and/or bitterness. Candace experienced this when she encountered one roadblock after another that delayed the rebuilding process for a full eighteen months.

Depending on the severity of the crisis and the community's long-term response capabilities, the disillusionment phase may last anywhere from a few months to two or more years, and it takes a tremendous toll. Families are at their greatest risk during this time, as coping resources are pushed past the breaking point.

Then, when those families finally come to terms with the limits of government and community assistance and gain renewed belief in their ability to take charge of their own lives, they enter the fourth phase.

4. *The reconstruction phase.* This is the equivalent of the acceptance phase in the grief cycle. In this phase, victims of disaster see external resources not as quick fixes but as tools to get them where they need to go. At this point, red tape and other roadblocks are tackled with renewed energy and persistence. During this phase, the family takes a decisive stance to work through their predicament.

For Candace, this meant becoming active in local politics to fight some of the city ordinances that were stonewalling her rebuilding efforts. During the reconstruction phase, external resources are still a vital part of recovery, but there is an emphasis on internal resources that makes recovery and reconstruction possible.

Helping Children Deal with Crisis

Unfortunately, when an earthquake or a fire or a flood hits, the disaster indiscriminately touches all who happen to be standing in its path—including children. Being caught in an earthquake or sitting in a storm cellar waiting out a tornado can be a traumatic experience for a strong adult. It can be absolutely devastating for a child.

So how do we respond to our children when we can no longer protect them from some of the harsher realities of life? Every family that has been touched by tragedy is forced to confront this heartbreaking reality. We experienced it ourselves when our son, Jeff, was diagnosed with a terminal illness, and there was nothing we could do to make it go away or stop the pain.

In times like these, how is it possible to help our children confront the harsher realities of life without taking away their faith and hope in its goodness? This is not an easy question to answer. In fact, it's a question that some of us have grappled with for years. But there *is* an answer.

The first thing parents must do in a situation like this is realize that their children are confronting such issues and that they need honest answers to their questions. Some parents make the mistake of ignoring their children's questions or trying to change the subject to something a bit more pleasant. But questions left unanswered will not go away with time, and for some children the concerns will persist and become debilitating in their frightfulness.

When disaster threatens young children, they come face-to-face with their own mortality, perhaps for the first time. Kids learn at an early age that pets and people die. But they don't see death as something that happens to them nor do they understand that it's a permanent state. It is only as we grow and mature that the nature of death comes into sharper focus. When young children encounter a traumatic life-threatening event, they come to see that not only could death happen to them and their parents but that it could happen at any moment in a violent manner.

Natural disasters thus force parents to validate their children's fears that bad and scary things do sometimes happen. But they don't happen every day, and it's important for parents to give their children as much honest reassurance as they can. Every parent would like to be able to tell his or her child, "I'll make sure that nothing like this ever happens again." But that's not the truth, because no one has that kind of power. It's far better to say, "I'm going to do everything I possibly can to make sure you are always safe." The second statement is an honest, reassuring pledge, but the first is a lie that can ultimately set your children up for feeling betrayed.

Surprisingly, you offer your children hope when you level with them, not when you lie to them. The truth is full of hope. It validates the fear that life is dangerous and unpredictable but also asserts belief in our ability to band together for safety and mutual encouragement.

It's harmful to obsessively worry about life's dangers, but it can be just as harmful to naively insist that no harm will ever befall us. When your children have been through a storm, you can calmly reassure them by acknowledging that, yes, the storm was scary and that some people were hurt. Fear can be abated when your children know that you take seriously the things that scare them but that you have come up with a plan to mitigate the danger if it should occur again.

If you are a parent, keep in mind that your children will pattern your behavior. If you overreact in certain situations, you can almost be certain your children will do the same.

A friend of ours recalls how thunder and lightning storms terrified her when she was a little girl. She and her best friend had heard horrible stories about people who had been burnt to a crisp as a result of lightning coming right through their open bedroom windows while they were asleep in bed. Sheila spent many summer nights listening for the sound of thunder so she could jump out of bed and close all the windows in the house before the lightning struck. She had also learned that "rubber acted as a grounding device," so she occasionally wore sneakers to bed. This behavior resulted in merciless teasing at the hands of her brothers and sisters, but it was the only way she could allow herself to fall asleep.

Now, certainly, lightning is nothing to sneeze at. An electrical storm *can* be dangerous, even though a person's chance of being hit by lightning is about the same as winning the lottery (in other words, extremely remote). But then again, because it can happen, a certain amount of fear might be considered healthy. In Sheila's case, this healthy fear had escalated to a frantic, near-hysterical level.

Unfortunately, her parents didn't know how to help her cope. Instead of sitting her down and having an honest and reassuring talk with her, they dismissed her fears, often yelling at her when a storm was approaching to leave the windows alone because the wind and the rain would help cool their hot and stuffy house.

It would have been so much better for Sheila if her parents could have told her yes, some people are killed in electrical storms, but most of those deaths occur outdoors. They could have told her that lightning was more apt to hit the trees outside than to strike their house—let alone come through an open window into her bedroom—and that there were other precautions she could take to prevent being "burnt to a crisp."

But her parents never did anything to help Sheila cope with her extreme fear, and as a result, she carried it with her into adulthood. She became edgy and upset every time the weather forecaster said there was even the slightest possibility of rain. She found herself battening down the hatches at the first sight of storm clouds and unplugging everything in her path to give the electricity "no place to run."

Her husband, Bruce, good-naturedly tolerated this behavior when it was just the two of them, but after their daughter Kaitlyn came along, he feared what Sheila's paranoia would teach their daughter. Sure enough, by the time Kaitlyn was three, Sheila and Bruce noticed that she started to cry whenever it began to rain. She had obviously picked up on her mother's fears.

Her panicked overreaction to electrical storms was instilling fear in her little girl, just as her parents' tendency to underreact and minimize her own fears had built up the terror in her when she was a little girl. You see, there is danger in overreaction, but there is also danger in underreaction. The proper approach is to meet your children's fears in an open, honest, and yet reassuring way.

As Sheila learned how to reassure her daughter that the rain wouldn't hurt her, that Mommy and Daddy know how to keep her safe, she was also reassuring herself. As Kaitlyn grows, she too will hear the tales of lightning gone wild, but she will be able to balance that with the other half of the truth modeled and spoken by her parents.

As the interaction with Kaitlyn illustrates, the level of our children's fears dictates the level of honesty and the type of reassurance they need from us. By the time a child is three or four, the concept of death may have entered their mind, but that does not automatically mean that this is the focus of their worries. They may be fearing for your safety or worried that they will be separated from you or a beloved family pet.

If your children are experiencing such fear, do your best to pay attention to the clues they are sending you. Ask questions about what they are thinking and feeling. Ask them to describe what is frightening them and why. Perhaps getting them to draw a picture or create a puppet show will provide young children with an alternate, less intense outlet for dealing with their fears and worries.

None of us have an easy time facing the harsher realities of life. Whether we've encountered natural or human-caused tragedies, life-threatening illness or random accidents, at one time or another almost all of us have had to find a way of sustaining hope in the midst of pain and tragedy. We can find peace and comfort by banding together in mutual love and support, not by hiding or running away from life's difficulties.

We have not been cast out into a cruel and dangerous world without God's provision of refuge and hope, without his direction and purpose. Our families will remain on the path that leads toward healing, so long as we claim for ourselves God's promises of love and comfort.

Seeking God's Response to Our Pain

The beauty and wonder of the world that surrounds us should rightfully cause us to pause and give thanks to God, the Creator. We stand in awe of nature's mystery and majesty. But too many of us are also aware of nature's deadly power. The rain and sun that grow our food can also destroy our lives. The forces that give rise to the beautiful mountains can also crumble our homes. The most innovative designs and the strongest of human-made materials cannot always withstand the forces of nature. The steady ground beneath our feet can give way in an instant when an earthquake strikes. The house that has sheltered our family for generations can be reduced to splinters in a matter of moments by the force of a tornado or hurricane. This is the hard reality of living in a world that is at the mercy of natural forces.

This is a great mystery. We know that God is the author of life, that the Lord sets all things in motion. Perhaps it's easier to understand it when other people hurt us than when the forces God created seem to turn on us. We may be tempted to wonder why God didn't create a world that offers us more protection from the natural elements. But we know that God does not control the natural world as if it were his puppet. God does not send the bolt of lightning that starts a fire, but neither does God prevent it from causing damage.

Some speculate that when sin entered the world, all of creation was altered, setting in motion the natural hazards that have plagued humanity's safety since the dawn of time. For some, theological answers regarding nature's violence are not as clear. The only thing we can truly know as we live in this sometimes-difficult world is that we can trust God as both the author and sustainer of our lives.

Once again we find that God does not answer all of our why's, but rather responds to our pain and distress. God is there to walk with us through the trials and tribulations of life and give us what we need when we need it. Sometimes we just need to learn how to listen for God's response.

Throughout this book, we've talked a lot about utilizing internal resources. These are God's gifts waiting for you to claim. We've also talked about building and relying on the support of family and adoptive kin. Within these external resources, God meets us in our pain and responds to our needs.

God's response to tragedy will often come in the form of renewed energy, hope, and comfort, through family, friends, and community resources. It comes through faith put into persistent, decisive action—through faith that takes hold of the words found in Isaiah 40:31: "But those who hope in the Lord will renew their strength. They will soar on wings like eagles; they will run and not grow weary, they will walk and not be faint."

14

The Evil Within

A young woman is murdered. And a young man is arrested for her killing.

His parents can't believe he committed such a brutal crime. They promise to stand beside him, to do whatever they can to see the real killer brought to justice. But then evidence turns up that seems to suggest that he may, indeed, be the killer.

What do the parents do? Do they stand by their son whatever happens? How do they cope when the entire community turns against them? Can it possibly be true that their son is a murderer?

Does it sound like a movie plot? It is—from the 1996 film *Before and After,* starring Meryl Streep and Liam Neeson. But it is a plot taken from real life.

It's no secret that terrible criminal acts happen in this world every day. Walking among us are murderers, sexual abusers, robbers, drug dealers, all sorts of criminals, some of whom victimize and hurt others without giving it a second thought.

And the truth is that the direct victim of a crime or an abusive act is not the only one to suffer. There are other, silent victims, as well. These are the family members of those accused and/or convicted of acts of cruelty against others. This point was driven home by another thought-provoking 1996 movie, *Dead Man Walking,* which explored the effect of a terrible double murder on both the victims' families and the criminal's family—showing the pain and sorrow that had come to both.

Finding out that someone in your family has committed a crime or has been charged with a crime can be devastating. If such a thing should happen to you, you are likely to be caught in a sea of conflicting emotions: disgust toward the violent act, sorrow for the victims, disbelief and shame that someone you love could do such a thing, humiliation as the family name is publicly dishonored by the evil acts of one member, and feelings of guilt by association.

Any one of these emotions by itself can be overwhelming. Your disgust and sorrow may lead you to disown the family member involved. Your disbelief may lead you to defend and cover for the perpetrator, standing up for him or her despite overwhelming proof of guilt. Or your shame, humiliation, and guilt may lead you to withdraw from the comfort and support you need to help you make your way to the other side of this family tragedy.

You may also be saddled with the added burden of legal fees and lost income if the perpetrator is incarcerated and was a major financial contributor to the family. You may feel alone and cast out as others seem to turn against you.

It is most difficult to know how to respond in such a situation. You are likely to be in shock and have the feeling that you are being pushed and pulled in several different directions at once.

If this should happen to you, the first thing you must realize is that when a family member perpetrates a crime against another, your entire family is also victimized. Your pain is valid. Your confusion is understandable. And for your family to heal, the pain must be tended to.

When you experience a crisis such as a family member's involvement in a violent crime, you are immediately thrown into the grieving process—passing through the various stages that were discussed earlier.

- When you first hear the news, you are likely to go into shock.
- In the denial stage, you will find yourself refusing to accept the family member's guilt.
- Next, your anger is likely to surface toward the family member involved or perhaps toward those who you feel have falsely accused your loved one.
- The bargaining stage is likely to follow, during which you look for quick fixes to help you "be done with this mess" or make promises that you will somehow manage to "make it all up" to the victims.
- You are likely to enter into depression when you come to see clearly the reality of what your family member has done and that only he or she can take responsibility for what has occurred.

As you pass through all these stages, you are likely to be grieved and deeply saddened. Your family will be forever altered. And yet, your future will be determined by how well you resolve your conflicting emotions toward the family member who committed the offense and how successful you are in finding a way to go on with your family life with grace and dignity.

Your future cannot stay fixed on the shame you feel about the family member who chooses to act destructively toward others. You cannot afford to allow this unfortunate act, no matter how devastating it might be, to become the defining moment for your family. You cannot allow yourselves to become "the criminal's family." There is much more to you than that, and one criminal act, no matter how ugly, does not outweigh the positive contributions that have been made for years by the other members of your family.

Tough Love Is Responsible Love

Perhaps one of the most common responses to the news that a family member has perpetrated a violent crime is denial of his or her guilt. It is certainly true that many people are falsely accused of crimes. This is a grave injustice and a crisis involving your family as the direct victim. But for the purposes of our discussion here, we are referring to situations where the evidence is overwhelming, where the guilt is known, or at least highly probable. Whether or not the family owns up to the crime, denial is the refusal to acknowledge that someone we love did something so horrible.

Denial and bargaining are likely to lead you to minimize the severity of the crime. You may go so far as to justify the perpetrator's behavior by claiming, "He didn't know what he was doing" or "Someone else provoked her" or "It was an innocent mistake." Most people are capable of becoming rather creative as they make excuses for violence that has crippled or destroyed others.

Sometimes people defend their family member because of the deep psychological turmoil raging within. They can't bear to tolerate the thought that their parent, spouse, or child committed such a horrendous act, because after all, "What would that say about me?" We're not talking about the public humiliation. We're speaking of that part of the internal core self which is influenced by, and perhaps dependent on, that family member remaining good, caring, giving, and trustworthy.

In the previous chapter, we talked about a woman named Belynda who made the painful discovery that her daughter had been sexually abused by her father. At first, Belynda felt so betrayed by her father's sexual abuse of her daughter that she didn't want to believe the girl's story. The same was true of Belynda's siblings. To admit their father's guilt would mean to lose the man as they had come to understand him. In fact, Belynda's brother never could come to accept his father's guilt, because the very prospect was too threatening for him to handle.

This is, perhaps, the most powerful force behind the inability to fully acknowledge a family member's guilt. Such guilt forces us to redefine who we are. It makes us take a look at the broken humanity that resides in all of us, including the people we love and admire. How can we love a father, brother, or son who ruthlessly kills innocent people? How do we resolve years of trusting in the goodness of our grandfather only to learn that for years he has been sexually abusing another member of the family? When such things come to light, how do we make sense of our lives? Of our family's history? What is to become of our future?

These are tough and painful questions, but most of the answers can be found by working through the process of coming to terms with what this family member has done. This is a matter of embracing both love and justice, of recognizing that one without the other leaves each incomplete and distorted. Just as our full humanity is only realized as we commit ourselves to the process of reconciliation between God and one another, so too responding to the violence of a family member means believing in and being an agent of their process of reconciliation.

When we come before God, we know of our brokenness. We confess our failings and turn to him for the power to make our lives right. In the nineteenth chapter of Luke, we read about a tax collector who was notorious for the way he had exploited people. Upon hearing Christ's words, he responded by admitting his wrongs against humanity and vowing to do his best to undo them. Jesus greeted Zacchaeus' words with a warm embrace, announcing that "today salvation has come" to Zacchaeus' house.

It is out of God's love for us that we are led to confession and guided into taking responsibility for our actions. When Jesus accepted Zacchaeus' change of heart at face value, some people in the crowd began to mutter and complain. They weren't quite so ready to forgive. But Jesus told those "complainers" that he had come to seek out the lost in order to save them, not to condemn them. To save Zacchaeus, he first had to get the man to face up to his own guilt and, thus, to his need for redemption.

In the same way, if you truly love the "perpetrator" in your family, you will do what you can to guide him or her toward taking responsibility for what he or she has done. When you make excuses for his wrongs, or collude with her against authorities, you are not being helpful. Love is not asserting people's innocence in spite of their guilt. Love is helping them face up to what they have done, realizing that when they do, like Zacchaeus, they will gain their freedom, their self-respect, and perhaps even their salvation.

Loving a guilty family member is perhaps the toughest love of all. Such love involves communicating that because you love him, you believe in his ability to take responsibility for what he has done so that he may make peace within himself, with God, and perhaps even someday with his victims. It means being willing to risk his rejection of you by taking such a tough stand, since it may be the perpetrator's choice to refuse to face the truth. It also means recognizing that because of your refusal to protect and lie for him, he may be physically taken from your presence for a period of time—perhaps even for life.

Finding a Supportive Community

How you respond to the violent actions of a family member is only one piece of the recovery. Finding a supportive friend, family member, or community who can provide a shoulder to lean on is crucial. Sadly, in circumstances like this, you often find out who your true friends are. Some of those you thought were your friends are likely to judge you right along with the guilty party. Some may avoid you simply because they don't know how to extend a helping hand.

Renee shared with us about the scrutiny and gossip she was subjected to following her brother's conviction for a brutal crime. The whole town closely watched his arrest and subsequent trial. As mobs screamed for justice, she often feared that revenge would come in the form of harm to her or another family member. Reporters regularly camped out on her family's front lawn, thus stealing from her any sense of privacy. She often complained that her brother's actions seemed to give the world permission to destroy the lives of the rest of his family. She felt alone, and often, as she walked home from school, she was very scared.

This young teenager and her family had become isolated and ostracized by their community. They offered no excuse for the perpetrator's behavior, yet they were treated as though they were also guilty of the crime. To cope, Renee and her parents sought support from a church in a neighboring community. There, the youth group and an adult Bible study group embraced Renee and her parents. In the company of caring Christians they found a place to weep, to pray, to express their anger and outrage at their brother and son, as well as at the rest of their community. Through the loving support of a caring community, this family was able to find its way through a terrible tragedy.

Not everyone is victimized by an outraged community. Not everyone turns away from us when this type of tragedy strikes. But if your family is under increased stress as a result of some of these typical responses, remind yourself that you do not have to be a victim. Like Renee's family, you can take charge of your family's healing.

To do this, you may need to investigate the resources available in your community. For example, many prisons and social service offices offer support groups for inmate's families. Or it may simply be a matter of coming to trust the love and support that is already within your reach. Perhaps your own discomfort is sending out a red light, a "keep your distance" message. It may not be that your friends have deserted you but that they are trying to respect what they see as your wish to be alone. They may be waiting for you to give them the go-ahead that you need their company, or they may need you to show them how they can help you. Support may be as close at hand as simply asking a friend, "Can I talk to you?"

15

Thank You, Lord, for Each Other!

Unfortunately, there is no clear path to follow when it comes to recovering from acts of violence that have touched our families. But neither are we left alone in the dark. Our paths, though they may be unique, are illuminated to some degree by those who have traveled the road ahead of us. In their stories, we may see the many shades of our own pain and anguish and discover that there is hope for recovery. Just look around you and you will see the work of those who were compelled by tragedy in their own lives to reach out to help others. Mothers Against Drunk Driving is one example of this. There are literally dozens of others.

Many communities pull together in times of tragedy, instinctively knowing that it is in the company of others that we can find God's grace and healing. Whether we gather in public ceremonies or impromptu gatherings, the purpose is the same: to honor the dead and the wounded, to grieve in the company of others who care— all as part of the process of reclaiming new hope and meaning.

Not too long ago, we watched our country model the power of communal grieving in the days and months following the bombing in Oklahoma City. On the weekend following the blast, the city held a memorial service to honor the dead and injured, their families, and all those involved in recovery efforts. The entire community seemed to come together across lines of age, race, and economic status.

We listened as one speaker focused on the children of Oklahoma, talking about how, in an instant, their trust in the goodness of humanity was betrayed. She spoke about how one of the tasks of recovery is to teach our children that evil and violence are not the norm—something that may be hard to remember when you've been on the receiving end of someone's violent act.

How can we impart this life-saving, life-affirming message to our children when we ourselves are doubtful? During that same service, other speakers encouraged us to use our anger to seek justice, not revenge, to allow our pain to mobilize us to action that we might honor our loved ones' lives. We hear the apostle Paul admonishing us to overcome evil, not by returning evil but by doing good. This is what begins to happen when we stand together in mutual support and encouragement, when we grieve together and help each other as we travel the long road back to normal. It continues to happen as we trust that God, as we work through the healing process, can relieve us of the hate we harbor toward our aggressor.

If you are a survivor of loss from a traumatic incident, you carry a great responsibility toward your children. They turn to you to make some sense out of what happened, for reassurance that the world isn't really so bad, and for direction as to how to pick up the pieces and continue with their lives. If you have been touched by such loss, our prayer for you is that you will continue along on your path toward healing. We pray that you will seek out friends, family members, and supportive others with whom you can share your story and, in so doing, release some of your pain. In that community of support, we trust that God will provide you with direction, renew your hope, and restore your faith in humanity and in the goodness and beauty of the life that is ours through Christ Jesus.

Debilitating and Empowering Responses

In previous chapters, we have examined the impact of trauma on our families. Whether you're a direct victim, a "near victim," or a member of a victim's supportive community, whenever your safety has been compromised or your loved ones have been hurt in some way, you will experience this trauma on a cognitive, emotional, and physical level.

There are several different ways children and adult victims of traumatic experiences react to such post-traumatic stress.[11] While these various coping styles initially help, eventually they outlive their usefulness and can become harmful.

1. *Denial.* This style tends to show itself through such things as daydreaming, blocking of memories, staying busy, or flat-out refusing to admit that it hurts, as in, "Oh, I'm fine. It doesn't bother me at all."
2. *Withdrawal.* Trying to remain invisible is one of the characteristics of this coping style. For example, when teenagers distance themselves from friends or when adults try to avoid coworkers, spouses, and parents.
3. *Cut-off.* This coping style is designed to protect oneself from uncomfortable and confusing thoughts and feelings. This person may appear happy-go-lucky, or blank and dull, but whatever her style, she

will keep her emotional distance and put up barriers others cannot penetrate.

4. *Blame-taking.* Being a victim sometimes leads to a self-blaming style. This may be one's sacrificial attempt to make sense of a tragedy. Sometimes this style serves to protect others from the hurt and anger this person feels toward the one who caused the pain.

5. *Approval-seeking.* If an abuse victim or survivor can be "perfect" or admired at home, school, or work, then it reassures him that he is okay, that he is loved. This person works hard at making himself acceptable to others.

6. *Acting Out.* Misbehavior and other destructive behaviors are this person's way of coping with anger, frustration, and shame. When left unattended, such a response can lead to physical or verbal attacks and acts of vandalism.

When your family goes through a traumatic event, it is likely that each member of the family will cope in a different way. But the most important thing to remember is that when family members respond to each other in a caring, proper manner, it can go a long way toward lessening the impact of extreme stress. It is a tremendous help when all the family members look for opportunities to reach out in love and in support of one another. Below, we've listed a few of the ways your family members can respond to each other when you are all dealing with post-traumatic stress.

1. If you are a parent, provide extra verbal reassurance and physical comfort for your children. Young children may want to nestle close to you when sleeping. Older children may simply want to sleep in their parents' bedroom for the first few nights

following a trauma. These are appropriate, though temporary, responses to traumatic stress. Take time out to verbally encourage each other, including your spouse. Extra hugs are important. So is engaging your children in physical contact play.

2. Allow all family members to know what has happened. While children should not be exposed to every detail of events that happened to someone close to them, they do need to know the essential facts. When events are kept secret, children know that something is going on. They can see it in your face and sense it in your hushed conversations with other adults.

3. Encourage all your family members to talk about what has happened. Younger children may need to talk repeatedly about the event or express their thoughts and emotions through various forms of play. This is their natural way of working through grief or fear, so encourage them to express themselves through playacting with puppets, dolls, or Play-Doh figures. Children may also enjoy expressing themselves through drawing or painting, so invite them to draw a picture of what happened or of what they're feeling. Older children and teenagers may be encouraged to journal or write a poem or a story. With your child's permission, share these creations with your immediate family. This gives positive feedback to the child and provides an opportunity for the other members of your family to mutually encourage one another. Talking about the event promotes healing simply by putting us in intimate contact with one another.

4. Temporarily relax the standard of expectations you normally have for yourself and others in relationship to job and school performance. Family members will naturally be distracted in the days and

weeks following a traumatic event. Children may have difficulty completing school assignments, home chores, and other responsibilities. That is to be expected. It is also to be expected that you may not be as efficient as usual in your work. For that reason, it's important to speak to your child's teacher as well as your supervisor or coworkers so they can understand why there has been a sudden change in performance. It is also helpful to reassure them that you are taking responsibility for working through the grief. While everyone's workplace is different, we have found that teachers tend to be supportive of struggling students, especially when they know what's going on.

5. Encourage active participation in household, work, and school responsibilities. Easily managed tasks help family members maintain a sense of competence, a feeling of being useful and alive. Inactivity reinforces the negative perception that life has no meaning or purpose and that we can't go on.

6. Maintain physical activity through exercise and play. Trauma-induced stress wreaks havoc on our minds and bodies. It zaps our energy and distorts our thinking. Physical activity enables our bodies to produce feel-good endorphins, which give us a natural high to counteract depressive symptoms that often surface after a traumatic event.

7. Be mindful of the body's need for proper rest and nutrition. When you are under stress, your body's reserves are taxed. You're prone to being tired, and your immune system is more likely to become compromised. This is also the time when you are likely to be tempted to let good health habits fall by the wayside. In addition to maintaining a balanced diet, avoid foods and drugs that act as stimulants or depressants. For example, when you are under

stress, caffeine can stimulate a body that is already kicked into high gear, nicotine can drain the body of nutrients that are essential for fighting the effects of stress, and alcohol abuse simply postpones the grieving process while aggravating depression.

If you are thinking that it will be added stress for your family to change its normal health habits during a time of stress, you should know that over the past decade, experts in the field of trauma-induced stress have concluded that, next to how we perceive the event, the factor that most influences how well we recover from stress is how we treat our bodies. There has never been a better time to turn over a new leaf.

Some Signs of Trauma

How do you know if you or your children have been seriously affected by a traumatic event? You can watch for some typical symptoms which signal that you or other members of your family need some assistance working through the trauma. Often, the supportive care of family and friends is all that's needed. Other times, skilled assistance from a trained counselor or your family physician is necessary.

The difficulty is ascertaining when that skilled intervention is called for. Unfortunately, we cannot offer you a timetable to follow or another way to tell you for certain when a critical point has been reached. Generally, the best idea is to call a local mental health agency, your family physician, or a school counselor for advice and direction. But here are some typical behaviors to watch for.

1. Children may show developmentally irregular behavior. Older children may regress to bed-wetting or soiling, thumb-sucking, or may act older than

their age. Adults may show a loss of confidence in their ability to function at work, in school, or in the home.

2. Children and adults may experience changes in daily habits and routines. They may undereat or overeat, suffer from insomnia or sleep much more than normal, be tormented by nightmares, be fearful about falling asleep, or may suddenly be neglectful or overattentive to grooming and personal hygiene.

3. Children and adults may be increasingly fearful—of the dark, of loud noises, by the prospect of being separated from other members of the family—or they may indulge in overly compulsive behavior such as constant bathing or rocking.

4. Children may begin to avoid situations that represent a threat to their safety or are reminders of the violent event. A child who has been sexually abused may suddenly fear dressing in front of others. He or she may refuse to change clothes in gym class, for example. If the abuse is occurring in the home, he or she may try to stay away from home by becoming overly involved in school activities. If the abuse is occurring via a relative or family friend, the child may seek to avoid contact by feigning illness, claiming to have excessive homework, or coming up with some other excuse. After the Los Angeles riots, many children feared leaving their homes, even when accompanied by a parent. Children affected by floods or violent weather often fear cloudy, rainy, or windy weather. Adults may fear returning to work, driving a car, or any activity that requires leaving home.

5. Children may show negative changes in performance and behavior. Their grades may begin to fall, and they may be involved in fights, demonstrate a negative attitude, or withdraw from normal activi-

ties. Adults may show a decrease in on-the-job performance and have a short fuse.

6. Children may show a negative change in the way they relate to their peers and siblings. They may be involved in fights or other acts of violence, or demonstrate excessive passivity, including withdrawal from social situations. Adults may experience increased marital tension and compromised ability to parent. Often, there is an increased risk for incidents of spousal and child abuse.

7. Children may be unable to concentrate on homework or other tasks, being easily distracted and fidgety. They may increase their television viewing because this offers an easy escape. Adults may ignore regular household chores or demonstrate extreme forgetfulness when it comes to deadlines and other obligations.

8. Children and adults may demonstrate distorted or dangerous thoughts, feelings, or behaviors. Drug and/or alcohol abuse is common following a traumatic event, as is delinquent behavior such as shoplifting and fire-setting. Children and adults may also express suicidal thoughts, suffer flashbacks, or engage in self-mutilation such as hitting themselves or banging their heads. Sometimes children blame themselves for the trauma another family member has experienced, believing that if they were only nicer or had not wished those mean things, nothing bad would have happened. Adults may also experience feelings of self-blame such as, "If I hadn't moved our family here, this wouldn't have happened." This involves an irrational belief that they could somehow have prevented the tragedy.

9. Children and adults may also experience physiological symptoms such as digestive ailments, including queasiness, stomachaches, vomiting, indiges-

tion, and bowel or bladder problems. Increased headaches may also occur, and children will often complain of simply not feeling good. Persistent itching and scratching and other skin disorders may also be experienced, and there may be dizziness and impairments in vision and hearing. Adults may also notice a decrease in sex drive, and women may experience painful menses or cessation of menses.

10. Watch for other signs of depression. In addition to the physiological symptoms mentioned above, other behaviors that indicate the presence of depression include withdrawal, overly compliant behavior, pervasive sadness, and hopeless or helpless beliefs and attitudes. Directly or indirectly, younger children may express their belief that life will never be safe or happy again, while teenagers may say they just can't cope.

11. Also watch for signs of anxiety in adults and children. In addition to the symptoms listed under numbers nine and ten above, anxiety may be indicated by excessive nervousness, irritability, hyperactivity, tics, obsessive thoughts, phobias (such as agoraphobia, which is a fear of open spaces), compulsive behaviors, and speech difficulties.

Moving Together toward Healing

While post-traumatic responses are often experienced off and on during the weeks and months following a tragic event, extreme symptoms will eventually subside as you work through your grief privately and in the presence of caring others. But just because you seem to be functioning better on the outside as time goes by doesn't necessarily mean that the pain is any less on the inside. In fact, as we've mentioned, you may carry the pain and sadness of certain events for the rest of your life. Grieving is the process of learning how to come to terms with the reality of a traumatic event, of allowing that event to become integrated with the rest of who you are in a way that does not control and limit you. As you pass through the grieving process, you will find that the intensity of the pain does lessen as it takes its place alongside the rest of the joys and sorrows of your life.

Before moving on, we offer three ways you and your family can actively participate in healing in the seasons ahead.

1. *Don't be surprised by seasons of sadness or mild depression months after a traumatic event.* It's natural for you and your children to experience an ebb and flow of painful emotions. Honor them and tend to them with loving care and patience. Talk with a friend who cares about you or take time to write down your thoughts and feelings. It's also good to go back and practice some of the empowering responses you offered one another when the initial event occurred.

2. *Event anniversaries and celebrations of other important dates associated with loved ones who have died are important markers.* Create a ritual of remembrance that has meaning for you and your family. Many churches and charitable organizations accept donations in memory of an event or the life of a deceased family member or friend. Do what you can to allow your family to remember. Public acknowledgment of your grief will remind you to stay in community with one another as you grieve.

3. *Create rituals of remembrance.* One couple that suffered major losses in a hurricane observed the one-year anniversary of the event by getting out photographs of the damage done to their home. While it was a somber occasion, it was also a time to cel-

ebrate their survival and recovery. Remembrance rituals allow us to focus on the bonds of love and support that have sustained us in the time following the ordeal. This should be a time of giving thanks to God for the gift of life and togetherness. You might want to host an informal barbecue, create a prayer service of thanksgiving, or simply pull a trusted confidant aside and quietly share your triumph of survival.

What we've attempted to do here is offer you a survival guide of sorts. Our intent is to provide you with a way of assessing the needs of your family and to give you some practical ways for responding in a healthy, positive way.

Each family and community tragedy, whether instigated by humans or by nature, carries a unique set of challenges. We encourage you to supplement what we have offered with other resources that address your particular needs in more detail. In appendix 1 you will find a sampling of resource books and organizations that provide a variety of services and materials for each member of the family.

You might want to check your local library, Red Cross, or social service agencies for materials pertaining to your specific circumstances. With more and more families having access to computer services, you may even be able to find what you're looking for on the Internet.

As with every traumatic stressor that affects our families, unexpected tragic events demand immediate and ongoing attention. A family faces its greatest challenge of survival in the aftermath of great pain and tragedy. Survival is not something that can be accomplished all alone. Rather, it is a process that calls for us to join with our family, friends, and other members of the community.

You may not have been able to escape harm, but with a little insight, a helping hand, and a determined spirit, you can choose to survive. With the love and support of those you gather around you, and with the help of community resources, your family can heal. By tending to your needs and the needs of your children, your hope and trust in God and humanity can be restored.

Time for Reflection

1. What natural catastrophes have you and your family encountered? Share your story with someone, and tell them how the event affected you and your family.

2. Life is full of both sorrow and joy. How do you resolve the harsher realities of life? As a result of the crises your family has experienced, have you noticed your children struggling with these issues? If so, how have you responded to them? What areas still might need special attention?

3. Share with others in your family a passage from Scripture that offers you assurance of God's comfort in times of pain or fear. Talk to each other about some of the ways you see God providing direction, assistance, support, and encouragement. Spend some time in prayer together, thanking Jesus for such signs of his love.

4. If your family has been hit by a traumatic event, describe the post-traumatic stress reactions you or other family members have experienced. How did you respond? Are any family members still suffering? How might you respond to their pain?

5. Take some time to go back over the list of responses to family stress reactions. Which items have you been able to use? Share other caring responses that are not listed, and add these to the list.

6. What is your immediate response to stress? Is your particular coping style an advantage or disadvantage to you? What can you do to temper your style so you are more effective?

PART 5

Step into the Future

16

Learning to Let Go of the Past

Does your past hurt?

When you look back on yesterday, is it with fondness—or dread? Do you see scenes that look like they could have been crafted by Walt Disney himself, or does your early life more closely resemble a movie that could have starred a fellow by the name of Freddie Kreuger?

More than likely, what you see is a mixture. Part dream, part nightmare.

But even if most of what you see is a sweet dream, there is likely to be some residual pain from the nightmare part. And the more your past resembles a nightmare, the stronger and deeper the pain is likely to be.

Whatever pain you are carrying, it is important not only for your sake, but for the sake of your entire family, that you seek out the healing you need.

Otherwise, something of the pain you feel, including your fears and anxieties, is likely to be passed on to your children.

How can you find healing for something that has hurt you for so long? Becoming whole is a process that involves spending some time focusing on a few specific tasks.

Steps toward Healing

Gathering the Courage for Self-Examination

Begin with taking the time to assess where you and your family are today. This first step toward healing involves courageous self-examination—looking inward to see how you are feeling, thinking, and behaving. It requires that you ask yourself some honest questions about how you are functioning in the world and about how your family is doing as well. It involves noticing how your behavior is affecting those around you—your spouse, your family, those you love, and even your coworkers.

To observe yourself and your family, you will probably need to learn how to sharpen your perceptions, which will then allow you to ask new questions. To understand who you are, you will need to somehow stand outside of yourself for a moment to expand your field of vision.

How can you do that? For starters, you can read books like this one, which should help to shed some light on areas of your life you may have never thought about before. You can also gain a new perspective through talking to others and listening openly to their perceptions. You can learn much about yourself and your family by participating in group or individual therapy. Therapy is most helfpul in that it invites a neutral observer to enter your life and help you see yourself more clearly.

Taking Time to Grieve

The second step toward healing is the grieving of past hurts. Healing will come as you move through the grieving process. So grieve for your lost childhood; grieve for the pain that went unnoticed by your parents; and grieve even for the pain you saw in your parents. Taking the time to grieve is a crucial step that allows you to begin letting go of the past. As you work through this process, your past can then become something that informs your present—as opposed to something that controls it.

Different people grieve in different ways. Some do it quietly in private. Others need to talk their way through it. Most people need a proper balance—a time when they can be alone with their feelings and a time when they can share with others what they're thinking and feeling. The healing process for you and your family is certainly enhanced when you share with your spouse and other family members what you are going through. As family therapists, we have often witnessed the beauty and power of families who have worked through their grief together.

Owning Your Actions

The third step toward healing is to take responsibility for your present behavior. Something interesting is likely to take place within you as you examine how your past has influenced your present. You will begin to understand more clearly why you do the things you do. You'll see certain roles you play in your family and other relationships, as well as myths you have come to believe about yourself and others.

Oftentimes, you will see how your behavior tells a story of unmet needs, of fears, and of resentments you're trying desperately to resolve. You can't leave it there, though. Your grieving of the past and gaining insight into your behavior will have no significance or purpose until you take the next step—and change your behavior.

You will come to see at this point that the tears you shed for your past pain were not in vain and that you are finally living in the present!

Coming to the Place of Forgiveness

The fourth step toward freedom from the pain of the past involves forgiving those who have hurt you.

It's important to understand exactly what forgiveness is. Sadly, it is often completely misunderstood by well-meaning Christians.

Some people are quick to offer a perfunctory "I forgive you," but they don't really mean it. They say it because it is expected or perhaps because it makes them look better than the person who has offended them. But when you say, "It's okay," before it really *is* okay, you haven't dealt with the real feeling or the real resentment and anger. Left inside you, resentment and anger will only get worse over time, finally getting to the point where they fester and poison your entire system—like a splinter left in a finger. Forgiveness is more than giving lip service to a few magic words.

On the other side of the issue are those who insist on holding on to their hurts, who have the attitude that "after what you've done to me, I will never be able to forgive you." Certainly some actions are hard to forgive, especially wrongs that were committed intentionally and apparently without remorse.

But remember, forgiving someone does not mean you are condoning his or her actions, nor does it mean that you have to grin and bear it without expecting anything from the offending party. There is a tremendous difference between forgiving behavior and enabling behavior. It's never all right to hurt another person. To forgive someone does not mean to forget what he or she did nor to ignore the affect that person's wrong behavior has had on your life. If someone accidentally steps on your foot and breaks a toe, it may be easy to forgive, but you still need to seek healing for the injury.

Forgiving someone doesn't mean you have to like or trust that person. Forgiveness does not imply or require reconciliation. The person who has hurt you may never change, may never even admit to having done anything wrong, and so may still be dangerous. To forgive does not mean releasing someone from being held accountable for his or her actions.

Forgiveness can often involve a lengthy process. Many Christians think forgiving is always the first thing they should do, no matter what, but the truth is, it is often something that isn't fully realized until the end of a grieving process. It is only after you've undertaken a full accounting of how you have actually been wronged that you can come to understand what you are forgiving and why.

You will know forgiveness is present when you no longer want revenge. As Lewis Smedes says in his book, *Forgive and Forget,* you'll know you've forgiven your trespassers when you can "wish them well instead of harm."[12]

Forgiveness can take on many forms and can serve different purposes. For example, it is important to work through the process of forgiveness to reconcile relationships that are important to us. In such situations the trespasser genuinely repents: This person admits the wrong and sincerely tries to change—does change, in fact. Sincerity, combined with the trust that comes from changed behavior, moves us to forgive.

In situations like this, the one who hurts us is willing to take responsibility for what he or she has done. Forgiveness is worked out through the process of healing the relationship. It is the prerequisite to reconciliation.

Other times, the behavior of the offending party has caused irreparable damage to the relationship. In such instances, forgiveness can't be worked out within the context of the relationship because there is no relationship left. Instead, forgiveness is a process you must work through internally, away from the trespassing party, to experience God's healing in yourself. When you've been wronged, you're susceptible to letting hate and resentment build up and harm you. You may spend a good portion of your time fighting and raging uselessly against someone who is no longer even in your life. Forgiving is a major step toward releasing yourself from that person's harmful grip.

It may be that the person you most need to forgive is yourself. You may realize that due to the pain of your own past, you've inflicted pain on your spouse or children; so you don't feel justified in seeking relief for yourself. You may fear pointing the finger of blame at your parents because you know that means three fingers will be pointing back at you. But whether you are in need of forgiveness or are being challenged to offer it to another, the process involved will teach you something about grace.

No matter how undeserving you may feel, God is always ready to forgive and accept you. Once you have learned to rest in the Savior's forgiveness and acceptance, you will begin to heal. And then your gratitude for Christ's forgiveness will, in turn, inspire you to give back to him by reaching out to others—which is a true sign of repentance. Those who have sensed God's forgiveness, either internally or through the forgiveness extended to them from another, know the life-changing power of God's grace. When that happens—and when you have come to terms with your past and the wounds it has caused—you have been healed, and you will be free to move bravely into the future.

17

Endurance in the Face of Pain

What can you do to bring healing and healthiness to people in pain? A good place to start is to understand what Jesus meant in Matthew 19:19, when he commanded us to love our neighbors as much as we love ourselves.

Jesus told the parable of the good Samaritan in response to the question, Who is my neighbor? After contrasting the Samaritan's caring attitude with the indifference demonstrated by the Levite and the priest, Jesus asked, "Which of these three do you think was a neighbor to the man who fell into the hands of robbers?" When the answer came, "The one who had mercy on him," Jesus responded, "Go and do likewise" (Luke 10:29–37).

It would have been so convenient for us all if Jesus had made a clear distinction between those who are our neighbors and those who aren't. Instead, he made the startling assertion that every needy person is our neighbor. Thus, our calling is to do what we can to empower the family in pain to carry on, to give aid that fosters healing.

So we know now what we're supposed to do. But still the question remains, How do we do it?

The place to begin is to remove obstacles that prevent us from making a compassionate (proper) response.

Removing Roadblocks to Helping Others

Many times, we may withhold care for others because of a subtle belief that "they got what they deserved." The feeling is that "since their problems are the result of their own mistakes, they don't deserve my hope or compassion." We may think that people in trouble could have avoided their problems "if only": if only he had listened to the wisdom of others, if only she was strong enough to kick the habit, if only he had been wearing a seat belt, if only she hadn't been so promiscuous, and so on.

Instead of compassion, some people hurl ridicule and judgment. This is most evident in the way some Christians have responded to the AIDS crisis. But that's far different from the way in which our Lord responded to the pain and suffering of humanity. His response to pain ought to show us all there is no place in our hearts for a harsh, condemning attitude.

Jesus' acceptance of the sick and hurting should give us much to think about. His example of healing and then reintegrating social outcasts into society indicates that he rejected the concept of suffering as divine punishment. While Jesus taught that all people must turn away from their sins, he never withheld care and compassion from those who were suffering as a result of sinful choices.

The woman at the well is a prime example of this. The Pharisees judged her by her heritage as a Samaritan. Her own community may have judged her because of her moral failures. In any case, we can see that the woman was aware of her need by the fact that she asked Jesus to give her some of the "living water" he had told her about.

Jesus knew about her sins and made it clear that her lifestyle was aggravating her pain. We have no idea how this woman ultimately responded to Christ's words. We know she brought many people to hear him speak, but the Bible doesn't say if she really made the necessary changes in her life. What we do know is that Jesus was unconditionally compassionate and loving toward her. He did not treat her as if she were a failure, an outcast, someone who was filthy and disgusting. Instead, he spent time with her, treating her with dignity and respect.

If you find that you are having a hard time letting go of a judgmental attitude toward those who are hurting because of their own behavior, ask the Lord to change your heart. Perhaps it would help you to undertake a study of the life of Christ, to pattern your own behavior more carefully after his.

Listening with Compassion

Once those roadblocks are removed, one of the most powerful ways you can help people who have been traumatized is to listen to their heartaches. Listening is a basic communication skill, yet so many of us still do not know how to listen effectively. The following is not intended to be a how-to list—something that should be memorized or followed exactly—because if you were spending all your time trying to remember what came next on such a list, you really wouldn't be listening anyway! So please consider the following to be helpful hints for how to offer a listening ear to people in pain.

1. Approach each person in need as if you've just entered a holy place. Each person's needs and preferences are unique, so allow her words and actions to be your guide. This means asking her if you can sit and talk with her for a while or if she would like you to hold her hand or offer a shoulder for support. These types of gentle questions allow the

other person to remain in control of the situation—deciding whether she wants to talk, whether she needs to be touched, where and when she is ready to share.

2. Listening doesn't involve solving a problem or taking the hurt away. It means walking beside someone who is in need, letting him know that you care about what he is experiencing, thinking, and feeling. It's letting the person in pain talk about what is important to him. It's giving him the freedom to vent, to explore ways of making sense of things, to cry, or even to be silent in the company of another person.

3. Expressing care through listening means accepting where another person is in her beliefs, reactions, and emotions. Her choice of verbal expression may not be what you are accustomed to. Her attitude toward God and others may not be kind. Her anger and grief may be deep and uncomfortable, especially if you have never experienced these emotions with such intensity. Occasionally, you may find that you have to keep your own emotions and reactions in check to continue in a helpful and open-minded attitude.

4. In responding to the pain of those you love, you should be watching for signs that more assistance or skilled help is required. Perhaps food, shelter, and clothing are needed. If that's the case, offering your assistance or help in steering them in the direction of appropriate services is the action part of listening. If you sense that someone is in danger—if his judgment is perilously clouded or he is engaging in irrational behavior of some type—seek assistance immediately. Enlist the help of another family member or friend, offer to spend the night, or call a family physician or coun-

selor immediately. Listening with an inner wisdom requires an ability to take concrete action in emergency situations.

5. Finally, when you offer a listening ear, you need to be aware of your limits. If you are tired or preoccupied, you'll need to arrange another time to talk. If you are emotionally distraught yourself, you need to admit that you're just not capable right now of giving the other person the undivided attention she needs. Perhaps the best way you can offer care at times like these is to be honest and, if you're able, guide her to someone who can give her the time and attention she needs.

You may feel inadequate in the face of another's pain. But in spite of the way you feel, our Lord may use you to bring comfort to those who need his touch. We are reminded of the loving care God gave to the children of Israel: "It was I who taught Ephraim to walk, taking them by the arms; but they did not realize it was I who healed them. I led them with cords of human kindness, with ties of love; I lifted the yoke from their neck and bent down to feed them" (Hosea 11:3–4).

Healing Rituals

When you allow your friends to vent the stressfulness of their circumstance and freely express their emotions, you offer them a place of healing. In addition to this, as we have discussed previously, it is often helpful and supportive to use rituals and symbols to help people deal with loss.

Think of the daily, weekly, and yearly rituals that are common in our culture. Daily routines include having an evening or morning prayer, saying grace before meals, and tucking the children in at bedtime with a story or song. Weekly rituals include worship services for confession and renewal before God and one another. Yearly rituals include celebrations of birthdays and holidays, and there are also weddings and funerals that signify beginnings and endings. All of these rituals help us mark past, present, and future traditions and give us an opportunity to reflect on the meaning of these events.

Rituals such as these can be especially helpful for people going through stressful times, because they provide a way to signify the loss and pain, to express regret regarding what has happened, and to prepare for the future. The elements of the Lord's Supper illustrate how focusing on the past can also give promise for a new future. People need a place and time for endings so they can move on to the possibility of new beginnings.

The Endurance That Brings Hope

When tragic loss strikes, we may feel without hope in the painful circumstances of life. We may ask ourselves a myriad of questions regarding why this had to happen, especially why it had to happen to us, and why we feel such pain. We are promised abundant life, and yet we suffer greatly in this life. The words "all things work together for good" are not very satisfying when you are in the middle of excruciating circumstances.

It is right to protest the fallen conditions that contribute to the pain in this world. It is right to rage against injustice, war, sickness, disease, brokenness, damaged emotions, poverty, and death. The pervasiveness of evil permeates our entire social structure, and we are right to make every attempt to save life, to heal brokenness, to work toward peace and justice, to do whatever we can to eliminate poverty and the other ills of our world.

It is both a right and a responsibility to take action whenever we experience pain or see it in the lives of others. To do less would be to fail our destiny as God's children. We are called to do what we can to bring hope to our hurting world. At the same time, we must recognize our human limitations and acknowledge that authentic healing and wholeness can be found only in Christ, who truly is the solid rock on which we stand.

Sometimes, people succumb to their problems when what they really need to do is roll up their sleeves and wrestle with God about their plight. Like Jacob, who would not let go until he received a blessing from the angel, we too must persist. For when we stay with it, stubbornly hanging on to what we know to be the truth, we have the chance to come to God on a more intimate level. When you wrestle with God about your predicament, you discover God; and in that discovery you are blessed, even in your pain.

Author Frederick Buechner expresses such a discovery in his own life. "I learned something about how even tragedy can be a means of grace that I might never have come to any other way. As I see it, in other words, God acts in history and in your and my brief histories not as the puppeteer who sets the scene and works the strings but rather as the great director who no matter what role fate casts us in conveys to us somehow from the wings, if we have our eyes, ears, hearts open and sometimes even if we don't, how we can play those roles in a way to enrich and ennoble and hallow the whole vast drama of things including our own small but crucial parts in it."[13]

Defeating the Despair of Pain

We can foster hope in ourselves by recognizing the glimpses and signs of God's presence during our times of trouble. A little boy in Sunday school was told that God would be with him when he was afraid. He was not comforted by that thought and protested, "But I need a God that's got skin on!" We all know that same feeling. We all need a God with skin on when we are frightened, hurting, or in despair—which means you need to see God in me when you're hurting, and I need to see God in you when I'm hurting. When we comfort one another with compassion and concern, we remind each other of the very real presence of God.

Let Judy tell you about a time she received a glimpse of God's loving care during our son's terrible illness.

I had spent a month with Jeff at the National Institute of Health in Bethesda, Maryland, and had just been told that his prognosis was very poor. He probably had only a few more months to live. God had not answered our prayers for healing, and I was overwhelmed by grief. Yet I needed to fly home for my daughter Jacque's eleventh birthday. Jacque had been staying with relatives all summer, and I knew she needed to have me home for awhile. It had been a tearful airplane trip; for once I got away from the hospital, I crashed under the weight of the dreadful situation, and the flood of feelings I had kept back broke through the dam. I walked off that airplane in pretty bad shape, wondering if I'd have the strength to drive the eighty-mile trip home.

To my surprise, my friend Dale was there to greet me. She became my strength and fortress. She took me under her wing, drove us home, and allowed me to vent the pent-up feelings. Then she helped me plan a birthday party for my daughter—a task that had seemed impossible in light of Jeff's illness. My friend Dale was my "God with skin on" that week. She brought me a glimpse of God's blessing and made it possible for me to be present with Jacque. I will never forget Dale's love. Even today, so many years later, I still thank God frequently for the way she blessed me. Her act of love gave me the assurance that Christ was with me. These bits of hope are an important part of the recovery process when we're in pain.

Forgiveness: Deflating the Power of Pain

We've talked throughout this book about the role forgiveness can play in bringing healing from pain. True forgiveness can free you from the bitterness and hate that can so easily rob you of life and joy.

Even as Frederick Buechner suffered the wounds of the memory of his father's suicide, he learned to free himself from the negative power of this woundedness through forgiveness.

We cannot erase the wounds that we suffer, he writes, but we can remove their power to hurt us and stunt our growth. The forgiveness of sins is "the interplay of God's forgiveness of us and our forgiveness of God and each other. To see how God's mercy was for me buried deep even in my father's death was not just to be able to forgive my father for dying and God for letting him die so young and without hope and all the people like my mother who were involved in his death but also to be able to forgive myself for all the years I had failed to air my crippling secret so that then, however slowly and uncertainly, I could start to find healing. It is in the experience of such healing that I believe we experience also God's loving forgiveness of us, and insofar as memory is the doorway to both experiences, it becomes not just therapeutic but sacred."[14]

Where are you in the process of letting go of anger, hate, or feelings of revenge? If you are struggling with such emotions, talk about them with friends and family members. Are those feelings interfering with your recovery from pain, with your ability to be there with and for other members of the family? It would not be possible to overstate the importance of forgiveness.

Lord Give Me Patience—Right Now!

Patience is one of the most important tools for successfully facing the challenges brought by tragedy, pain, and loss.

We remember watching as Jacque, who was then three, bent down for what seemed to be the two-hundredth time to examine another ordinary rock as we went on our daily walk. How amazed we were by her desire to take in the wonder of every bit of life she could see, smell, or touch. Turning a piece of bark over to find tiny bugs, throwing a rock in the water to watch it ripple, noticing the colors of an interesting leaf—all such things were a part of her unhurried world. We remembered how someone told us that a small child can easily complete a walk of three miles as long as you're willing to go at her pace. We had to learn to be patient if we were going to share the fascinating discoveries and marvelous adventures of our daughter's world.

But patience doesn't come easy. Being patient with ourselves and our families is one of the most difficult parts of going through various life stages. We get caught up so easily in the tyranny of life's stressors. We are often tempted to define ourselves by the world's standards of productivity, losing sight of our step-by-step walk with family members. We must constantly remind ourselves that developing character takes a willingness to let go of the urgent, which can rob us of so much that is truly important.

One father told us that he had found himself constantly waiting for his children to outgrow each difficult life cycle—3 A.M. feedings, diapers, tantrums. Then one day he realized that he was missing the uniqueness of each day, a period in his family's life that was new and would be gone tomorrow. He learned to slow down and enjoy the beauty and wonder of each day.

Some of us don't have a great deal of trouble being patient with others, but we really struggle with patience where our own weaknesses are concerned. A friend of ours who has gone through a long process of suffering with mental illness remembers crying out, "How long, O God?" Her family, her church community, and her friends were deeply involved with each success and failure. When she came through another crisis, it was cause for celebration; when she went through her deepest despair, it took all levels of the system to support her. All of those who walked along the difficult path with her learned much about the faithful presence and patience of God.

Sometimes a person under stress becomes her own harshest critic. She may get mad at herself for crying or losing her temper; or she may even punish herself with thoughts such as "I'm such a failure" or "I always mess things up." It is tragic that we're so hard on ourselves, because we are all human and as such are prone to make many mistakes. Only one perfect human has ever walked this planet, and that was nearly two thousand years ago.

So have patience with yourself! Recognize that new and difficult challenges are bound to throw you off track at times. Recognize that your mind, body, and emotions have their limits and that exhaustion can overwhelm you. Reassure yourself that you can survive life's challenges—because you can. You can learn and grow amid the confusion and chaos. Ask God to help you have a proper perspective and to be patient and gentle with yourself when you ought to be. As God answers that prayer, you will begin to take responsibility for your life, and that is when your shortcomings will become opportunities for growth in wisdom instead of occasions for self-flagellation.

Remember, God doesn't hurry people. The children of Israel wandered in the wilderness for forty years. Abraham and Sarah waited for their promised child for more than twenty-five years. Sometimes God seems to be silent, but that never means Yahweh has turned away from you. Psalm 37:7 tells us to "wait patiently" for God. The time when you need to pay the closest attention to God's heavenly way is when you are distracted by the stressors of life.

Remember, though, that waiting does not necessarily imply inaction. Hannah persisted a long time before the Lord, weeping tears of bitterness in her desire for a child. She cried, she prayed, she struggled, she wrestled with God, and her son, Samuel, became one of Israel's greatest leaders.

Patience, the fruit of the Spirit, is a precious gift that is built in us when we learn to wait on God. As Isaiah 40:31 says: "But those who wait for the Lord shall renew their strength, they shall mount up with wings like eagles, they shall run and not be weary, they shall walk and not faint" (NRSV).

God is a faithful and merciful God, and the time you spend waiting on him will not be in vain!

God Cares about Your Pain

The Bible tells us that nothing that happens to us can separate us from the love of God (Rom. 8:38–39). Over and over again, God promises through the Holy Scriptures to be with us in every painful situation. He says:

> "Never will I leave you; never will I forsake you" (Heb. 13:5).
> "I am with you always, to the very end of the age" (Matt. 28:20).
> "Cast your cares on the LORD and he will sustain you" (Ps. 55:22).
> "Do not fear, for I am with you" (Isa. 41:10).

> "Cast all your anxiety on him because he cares for
> you" (1 Pet. 5:7).

Elsewhere in the Bible, God promises that we won't be
tempted above what we can handle (1 Cor. 10:13) and
that the water won't sweep over us or the fire consume
us when we pass through times of trouble (Isa. 43:2).
Because God has overcome the evils in the world (John
16:33), we can be confident that we will be delivered from
the tragic things that happen in our lives.

Surely it takes a special touch of God's grace for us to
be able to choose faith over despair when we are caught
in the middle of a painful situation. But the truth is that
God is there, our Lord does care, and knowing that can
go a long way toward eliminating fear and anxiety.

At this point it seems important to say that the crises
we pass through are not designed by God to rob us of
those we love, or of our comfort and security, to teach
us some lesson or bring us to wisdom. Although we may
suffer as a result of human error, we do not believe that
God doles out punishment to keep us on our toes. Even
when God uses the tragedies of our lives to change our
hearts, deepen our faith, and spur us on to action, we do
not believe that God has caused the suffering. Using it
and causing it are two very different things.

It is much easier to deal with unfair tragedies when we
understand that God is for us in the midst of the suffering. Often, in the pain and suffering that pound away at
us, the certainty of God's love is all we can hold on to.

And in the midst of turmoil, it is often others who keep
us holding on to God, who pray on our behalf when we
are too numb, immobile, or unable in some other way to
pray for ourselves. Our family and friends can hold on to
hope for us when we are ready to let go. Judy will never
forget how her students surrounded her with their loving prayers during her mother's illness. Their sensitive

faith brought reassurance of God's infinite and active presence.

When you are crushed in spirit, you need a peace that surpasses your human understanding of things. You need the assurance that God can meet you where you hurt, deliver you from your fears, and be your refuge in time of trouble.

When you recognize your need for others in your time of pain, you have come to the heart of the matter. It is then that you enter that inner sanctuary of vulnerability. For when we face each other unafraid and embrace each other's pain, courage is born. In our connectedness to others, we meet our Creator face-to-face, finding ourselves stripped of all defenses and pretenses and coming to know ourselves more fully than ever before. This is when we hear God's voice more clearly, enter his rest more fully dependent upon Jesus, and find healing for our pain.

By sharing in the struggles of others and letting ourselves be affected by their pain, we actually participate in the elements that define our humanity as being created in the image of God. You see, loss brings home to us the terror of separation. When all is right with our world, we feel safe and loved; but when that safety is threatened, we must face the terror of aloneness. We instinctively know that this separation can lead ultimately to death.

We are threatened constantly with separation because we live in a fallen world. It is this agonizing condition of separation that fills God's heart with compassion toward us. God became flesh and blood and shared in our suffering to put an end to our separation from him and from each other. God not only felt for our pain but experienced it through the incarnation. The greatest comfort in the world will come to you when you truly realize that Jesus shares in your pain. That is when you know for certain you are not alone!

Philippians 3:10 tells us that if we would truly know Christ, we must share in his sufferings. And, remember, Jesus' sufferings came as a result of his sharing in our pain! To be truly human, we're called to share in the sufferings of one another just as Christ shared in our sufferings. It is through caring that we give life, that we come to truly know Christ and one another.

Loss forces us to feel our incompleteness and vulnerability. When caring others empathize with our pain, it no longer has the power to destroy us. That is how empowering care heals. The power of a listening and caring heart doesn't fix the problem, turn back the clock to better days, protect the future, or stop the pain. But it does give hope and life, as the one in pain realizes that he or she is no longer alone.

A Personal Note

We were privileged to have, for ten years, a son who filled our lives with love, excitement, and humor. Jeff died a few days short of his tenth birthday, after a three-month fight with cancer. Although the pain of his death is still with us, the sting of the loss has lessened with time.

One evening, lying on the living room sofa (which had been his bed for a month), Jeff suddenly said to Judy, "Mom, I'm going to die! Mom, I'm going to die!"

Jack sat down on the bed next to him to try to comfort him.

"Dad," Jeff said, "I'm going to die!"

"I know, Jeff," Judy said.

"Is that okay? How long will it take?" he asked.

Throughout his illness, Jeff was very much aware of his closeness to God and totally secure in the love of Jesus Christ as his Savior. We assured him that we were ready to let him go and that he would be in the arms of Jesus, all of us sensing that this would be the last evening we would spend together as a family. Calmed by that reassurance, Jeff's anxiety quickly departed. That night our little boy died, peacefully, in his sleep.

A few days after Jeff's death, we were cleaning out the drawers of his dresser. There we found a little green Gideon New Testament in the back pocket of a pair of his jeans. Inside the front cover he had written, "I LOVE GOD!" When we opened the Bible, we found a note he had written sometime before he became ill. In his childish writing, it said, "I love you, Mom and Dad, even when you get mad at me. I will always love you."

That was a gift of unconditional love from him to us.

Even as we write this, some twenty years later, we still feel the sadness of our loss. And yet we know the healing that has come from our healer. We have learned that surely it takes a special touch of God's grace for us to be able to choose faith over despair when we are caught in the middle of a painful situation. But it is important to hold on to his promises, to know that God cares.

An enduring HOPE DEFEATS the despair of pain,
An enduring FORGIVENESS DEFLATES the power of pain,
An enduring PATIENCE DISCLAIMS the permanence of pain,
An enduring FAITH DISTILLS the potency of pain,
An enduring PEACE DELIVERS from the grip of pain!

APPENDIX

1

Where to Go for Help

Many of the support groups listed below generally offer free group meetings for individuals coping with a variety of painful issues. Also, many of these organizations offer educational materials, including books, films, and brochures.

Most self-help groups (see second half of listing) are based on the Twelve-Steps and Twelve-Traditions models originated by Alcoholics Anonymous.

The quickest way to locate the group nearest you is to check the white pages of your telephone directory, your local newspaper (call them if you don't see any listings), local hospital social service department, community service agencies, high school guidance counselors, or mental health professionals. The national offices can help you locate the group nearest you if this information is not listed elsewhere.

For Twelve-Step recovery groups, we also recommend that you check with local churches. Many support groups offer "general" Twelve-Step groups, but group support based on a Christ-centered Twelve-Step program can be inclusive for many issues pertaining to recovery, from childhood abuse to coping with adult life difficulties.

Grief Support

American Association of Suicidology
2459 South Ash Street
Denver, CO 80222
(303) 692-0985

The Compassionate Friends
Box 3696
Oak Brook, IL 60522-3696
(708) 990-0010
(312) 323-5010
(A support group for bereaved parents.)

Parents of Murdered Children
100 East 8th Street
Cincinnati, OH 45202
(513) 721-5683
Source of Help in Airing and
    Resolving Experiences (SHARE)

Saint Joseph's Health Center
300 First Capitol Drive
St. Charles, MO 63301
(314) 947-6164
(This organization helps parents who have lost a baby due to miscarriage or stillbirth and parents who have lost an

infant to connect with support groups and other resources.)

Coping with Terminal Illness

National Association of People with AIDS: (202) 493-3708

The Candlelighters Foundation
Childhood Cancer Foundation
2025 Eye Street, N.W., Suite 1011
Washington, DC 20006
(202) 659-5136
(Nonprofit organization of parents who have or have had children with cancer. Offers support groups, reference materials, and other support services.)

The Self-Help Center
1600 Dodge Avenue, Suite S-122
Evanston, IL 60204
(This center offers assistance in finding local support groups for all seventeen disease categories recognized by the World Health Organization.)

SIDS Alliance
10500 Little Patuxent Parkway,
    Suite 420
Columbia, MD 21044
(800) 221-7473
(This national office assists parents who have experienced the death of a child due to Sudden Infant Death Syndrome in locating various types of support services.)

General Support for Parents and Children

Parents without Partners
7910 Woodmont Avenue, Suite 1008
Bethesda, MD 20814
(301) 654-8850
(This organization offers support services to single parents and their children.)

Self-Help Groups

Alcoholics Anonymous World
    Services, Inc.
P.O. Box 459, Grand Central Station
New York, NY 10163
(212) 686-1100

Al-Anon Family Group Headquarters
1372 Broadway
New York, NY 10018

Incest Survivors Anonymous
P.O. Box 5613
Long Beach, CA 90805-0613
(213) 422–1632

Childhelp, USA
6463 Independence Avenue
Woodland Hills, CA 91367
Crisis Hotline: (800) 4-A-Child
Office number: (818) 347-7280
(If you or someone you know is feeling overwhelmed by parental responsibilities, this 800 number exists to offer you immediate assistance as well as referrals to groups and organizations in your area who can provide further assistance.)

National Association for Children of
Alcoholics
31706 Coast Highway, Suite 201
South Laguna, CA 92677
(714) 499-3889

National Cocaine Hotline: (800) 638-8682.

National Self-Help Clearinghouse
Graduate School, City University of
    New York
33 W. 42nd Street, Room 1222
New York, NY 10036
(212) 840-1259
(Provides listings for those seeking to recover from a variety of addictive disorders, such as alcoholism, overeating, gambling, etc.)

Parents Anonymous
22330 Hawthorne Blvd., Suite 208
Torrance, CA 90505
(800) 352-0386 (24-hour hotline)
(This group offers member-led as well as therapist-led support groups for parents who have abused their children. Groups are also available

for, or often include, their spouses and children.)

Parents United
Daughters United/Sons United
P.O. Box 952
San Jose, CA 95108
(408) 280-5055
(If you have sexually abused a family member, you may be referred to this group that provides crisis and long-term support for families in which incest has occurred. Groups are led by lay-members as well as therapists. Services include groups for perpetrators and their spouses; groups for sexually abused children; medical, vocational, and legal counseling.)

Appendix

2

The Stages of Grief

As we discuss these stages, we want to acknowledge our indebtedness to Elisabeth Kübler-Ross,[15] whose work with the terminally ill has helped us understand what happens to people internally when they are grieving. Her work has been complemented by J. William Worden,[16] an expert in grief counseling, who has brought to our awareness the many tasks that must be worked through in order to adjust to loss. The work of these two individuals has made clear that, even though there are common elements to healing, grieving is not an orderly process with predictable stages. The following phases are experienced differently by different individuals and are often repeated numerous times throughout the journey to recovery. Still, an inscreased awareness and appreciation for the various tasks of grieving will enable us to care for ourselves, our families, and our friends with greater compassion and patience.

Stage One: Denial

The first response to any crisis is almost always to turn away from it, to say that it can't really be happening. Denial is a natural response to tragedy. It comes in many forms and is experienced in a variety of ways. Denial is what happens when your mind and body can't fully grasp or accept the reality of what has happened. You feel numb. You're in shock. You may experience uncontrollable bouts of crying, you may find that you are clinging to mementos related to the loss, or you may fall into long periods of quietness and withdrawal. Some people experience physical symptoms similar to an anxiety attack—tightness in the throat, choking feelings, and/or shortness of breath. Concentration is difficult, and there may even be a temporary blurring of vision. Sometimes denial takes the form of minimizing the importance of whatever loss has occurred.

Occasionally, our religious beliefs only add insult to injury, leading us to hide and pretend we're not really hurt or afraid when we are writhing in pain and terrified. We have somehow come to think it's a sin or a lack of faith to feel pain or fear or any other negative emotion, so we tend to hide them, even from ourselves. That's not at all healthy.

What is healthy is to allow yourself to accept the reality of what is happening, but that is sometimes a difficult thing to do. One reason why is that from the time we were very young, most of us were taught to deny our feelings: "Come on now, it doesn't hurt!" "Big boys (or girls) don't cry." "Keep your chin up." "Just whistle a happy tune." And so on. In this way, we learned to deny our pain and fear.

Now, please don't misunderstand. Denial is not altogether bad. It is initially a good thing because it gives us time to absorb and acccept difficult realities. But it is not possible to live in a constant state of denial. For instance, cancer cannot be denied. In our situation, Jeff quickly picked up on the inconsistent messages we were giving him when we were still in denial regarding his cancer. Our outside cheerfulness was an obvious attempt to cover our inside fears, and he saw right through it. Finally, he had had enough and asked why everybody was acting so happy when he was feeling so sick!

What an eye-opener that was. We needed to be real with him and not walk around with false happy faces all the time. Only when we were able to name Jeff's disease as cancer were we able to talk about the fear with him and then face the months of treatment that lay ahead.

Stress does not diminish because you deny it's there. It simply stays hidden and keeps you immobilized.

Stage Two: Anger

Once you break through denial and begin to face reality, the real pain of your loss will be keenly felt, and you may demonstrate it in a variety of ways—two of the most common being sadness and anger.

Anger can be particularly dangerous if you don't know how to handle it. It may strike out blindly at innocent bystanders. Or it may even lash out at people you love who have had nothing at all to do with your loss, including those who only want to support and encourage you.

People who are deeply angry may not even be aware of the emotion or of how it is being mishandled. It's important to remember that anger can be handled properly, that it is not, in and of itself, a bad thing. The Bible does not say that anger is a sin. It's only when anger causes us to react in improper ways that it crosses the line into sin. Jesus was certainly angry when he drove the money changers out of the temple, but that was a constructive act. He was angry when he cursed the fig tree that bore no fruit and, in his anger, gave us a lesson about the importance of faith.

Somehow, we've come to believe that a godly person is never moved to anger but always manages to meet life's frustrations with nothing more than placid calmness. The truth is, anger can be an important, informative emotion. It alerts you when your security is being threatened. Many wonderful things have been accomplished—great and beneficial movements have been started—by people who were justifiably angry.

Rather than forbid ourselves to be angry or say that we don't feel anger when we do, we need to strive to learn how to understand anger—to read it, control it, and express it appropriately so that it does not manifest itself in destructive ways.

If you are having trouble with anger, if you are expressing it in harmful and dangerous ways, then you need some help learning anger-management skills. Do yourself a big favor by gathering up the courage to find a competent counselor. Therapy is not for failures or weaklings. Rather, the person who knows when to seek professional help displays a great deal of integrity and courage. And it is never too late to learn how to deal with anger.

Stage Three: Making Deals

Almost all of us have tried to make bargains with the Lord at one time or another. We play the game of "If only." "If only you will help me get through this, Lord, then I promise I'll be a better parent . . . or spouse . . . or friend." And then there are all the other promises such as, "I'll start attending church more often," "I'll increase my giving," "I'll really start living for you," and on and on they go.

Bargaining is closely related to denial. Those who try to bargain to change their situation cannot quite accept the final reality of what is going on in their life. They haven't come to terms with their loss of control and inability to turn back the tide. Bargaining revolves around the notion that if I do something for God, he will give me what I want. This attitude is subtly present in those who believe their relationship with God offers them a shield against the tragedies of life. These people often crumble in the face of adversity, because it catches them off guard.

Sadly, this type of thinking has been encouraged in recent years by a number of different preachers and teachers who have spread the false message that the righteous never have any kind of trouble. That message stands in stark contrast to the words of our Lord, who told his apostles, "In this world you will have trouble" (John 16:33).

The tragic thing about this type of "theology" is that it piles self-condemnation on top of trouble for people who are passing through hard times. They believe they are being punished for some act of disobedience, when in fact, the truth may be the opposite.

A certain amount of deal-making can be a natural part of coming to terms with a painful loss, but the development of a deal-maker mentality can be dangerous.

Stage Four: Depression

After the initial shock wears off, after we stomp our feet in protest and then watch as all our bargaining chips fall by the wayside, terrible reality begins to sink in. The person who reaches this stage may feel betrayed by God, by other people they thought they could trust, or by life itself. Reality can be a terrible blow, and its weight can fall in the form of dark depression.

Depression takes many different shapes. Sometimes it is a mixture of other feelings—anger, sadness, frustration, confusion, and guilt. The person who is depressed may have little or no energy, and may find that all of the things that used to give pleasure are now dull and lifeless. Depression may manifest itself in overeating or in loss of appetite. The depressed person may want to sleep all the time, or he may throw himself into his work with boundless energy to avoid thinking about things.

A certain amount of depression during a time of loss is natural. It is part of the mourning process. But it should begin to lift as time goes by.

Like anger, depression can be dangerous, especially if it becomes a hopeless, helpless feeling that lingers or that tempts you to hurt yourself. If you are depressed to the point that you feel there is no reason to go on living, then you definitely need some professional help.

Stage Five: Acceptance

Acceptance is the light at the end of the tunnel. To accept what has happened is to begin to move toward the future. It is an understanding that life has changed—perhaps forever—but that the world has not ended. When you are able to accept your loss, you are one step closer to being able to resolve it. This doesn't mean that the pain has gone away, but it does mean that the hurt is no longer so intense that it consumes you.

How can you get to the place of acceptance? Only by working through your feelings instead of running away from them.

After a death, some cultures stop all the clocks to symbolize that life as we know it has come to a halt. In a sense, then, acceptance is a restarting of your life's clock, a moving forward with life. It is a redirection of energy from mourning to the pursuit of living. It is a letting go of the past to embrace the future.

A word of caution: Embracing the future is not the same as trying to form relationships or make choices to run away from the pain of loss. We all know about romances that didn't work out because they were formed "on the rebound." Any relationship that is initiated as a means of escape from pain is pretty well doomed from the start.

Notes

1. B. Carter and M. McGoldrick, *The Changing Family Life Cycle* (Boston: Allyn and Bacon, 1989).

2. Erik H. Erikson, *Childhood and Society* (New York: W. W. Norton & Co., 1950).

3. J. I. Clarke and C. Dawson, *Growing Up Again: Parenting Ourselves, Parenting Our Children* (San Francisco: Harper & Row, 1989).

4. J. O. Balswick and J. K. Balswick, *The Family: A Christian Perspective on the Contemporary Home* (Grand Rapids: Baker, 1991).

5. See J. K. Balswick and J. O. Balswick, *Raging Hormones: What to Do When You Suspect Your Teen Might Be Sexually Active* (Grand Rapids: Zondervan, 1994).

6. See C. Penner and J. Penner, *Sex Facts for the Family* (Dallas: Word, 1992).

7. Wendy Fine Thomas, poem published in *The Stimuli,* a School of Psychology Student Publication, Fall 1990, p. 8. Fuller Seminary.

8. J. S. Wallerstein and S. Blakeslee, *Second Chances: Men, Women, and Children a Decade after Divorce* (New York: Ticknor and Fields, 1989).

9. Frederick Buechner, *Telling Secrets: A Memoir* (San Francisco: HarperSanFrancisco, 1991), 8–9, 21, 39, 22, 31–32.

10. Adapted by Colleen Jolly, Iowa State University Extension family life specialist, from materials for Outreach Iowa, August 1993. Outreach Iowa is a community-based crisis intervention, mental health treatment and training program, and project of the University of Iowa, School of Social Work.

11. J. T. Mitchell and G. S. Everly, *Critical Incident Stress Debriefing* (Ellicott City, Md.: Chevron Publishing Corporation, 1993).

12. Lewis B. Smedes, *Forgive and Forget* (New York: Harper & Row, Pocket Books, 1984), 29.

13. Buechner, *Telling Secrets,* 22.

14. Ibid., 33–34.

15. Elisabeth Kübler-Ross, *On Death and Dying* (New York: Macmillan Publishing Co., 1969).

16. J. W. Worden, *Grief Counseling and Grief Therapy* (New York: Springer Publishing Co., 1982).

Bibliography

Anderson, R. S. *On Being Human*. Pasadena, Calif.: Fuller Seminary Press, 1982.

Figley, Charles. *Helping Traumatized Families*. New York: Plenum, 1989.

Figley, Charles, and H. McCubbin. *Stress and the Family, Volume 2: Coping with Catastrophe*. New York: Brunner/Mazel, 1983.

Gilligan, C. *In a Different Voice*. Cambridge, Mass.: Harvard University Press, 1982.

Hill, R. *Families under Stress*. Westport, Conn.: Greenwood, 1949.

McCubbin, H. I., A. E. Cauble, and J. M. Patterson eds. *Family Stress, Coping, and Social Support*. Springfield, Ill.: Charles C. Thomas, 1982.

Vest, Norvene. "Broken and Shared: Discovering and Claiming My Own Holy History," *Theology, News and Notes* (June 1993): 18–21.